DIAMOND IN THE ROUGH

STRUGGLE OF SANKALP

AF570117

DR. SANKALP MIRANI

Copyright © Dr. Sankalp Mirani
All Rights Reserved.

This book has been published with all efforts taken to make the material error-free after the consent of the author. However, the author and the publisher do not assume and hereby disclaim any liability to any party for any loss, damage, or disruption caused by errors or omissions, whether such errors or omissions result from negligence, accident, or any other cause.

While every effort has been made to avoid any mistake or omission, this publication is being sold on the condition and understanding that neither the author nor the publishers or printers would be liable in any manner to any person by reason of any mistake or omission in this publication or for any action taken or omitted to be taken or advice rendered or accepted on the basis of this work. For any defect in printing or binding the publishers will be liable only to replace the defective copy by another copy of this work then available.

Acknowledgement

It's no secret that books themselves make me ugly cry and sob all the time. I've told you some of the top books that have made me cry and there have even been more since then...so it's clear I'm a crier when it comes to moving scenes in books. But I'm talking about something different altogether.

I have this fascination with the acknowledgements in the back of books. And I'm obsessive about reading them. Sometimes they are the pretty standard shout-outs but sometimes they make me feel an incredible surge of feelings and the swelling of my heart. And sometimes while I'm reading them I get all choked up, truly. Sometimes it's this whole little story in it of itself to me. There's just something incredibly personal and beautiful in some of these acknowledgements.

The world of a book, after all, is a private conversation between author and reader. Acknowledgments pages break that spell by bringing in the outside world. When agents and managers start to appear in acknowledgments, things get even weirder: here comes the world of commerce and deal-making, crashing the story party.

- "As he read, I fell in love the way you fall asleep: slowly, and then all at once." – John Green

"When I say I love you more, I don't mean I love you more than you love me. I mean I love you more than the bad days ahead of us, I love you more than any fight we will ever have. I love you more than the distance between us, I love you more than any obstacle that could try and come between us. I love you the most." – Sankalp Mirani

I Thank everybody who supported me in this venture

Can you put your hand in and give me hi-fi

How else i am supposed to thank you.

I am very much grateful to Andleeb and her team

for bringing my thoughts on paper and publish them in its true form.

I really appreciate my readers for sparing their valuable time and for the passion to know about Love ❤? and life which motivates me to keep on writing.

ABOUT THE AUTHOR

The author of searching and often dark meditations on universal themes, he is a quintessentially modern poet in his adherence to language as it is actually spoken, in the psychological complexity of his portraits, and in the degree to which his work is infused with layers of ambiguity and irony.

Sankalp Mirani paints a picture of a person who values her loved ones in her short, succinct bio. This gives the reader a comforting sense that the writer is compassionate, which is an attractive trait in a children's book author.

He describes the trajectory of his background that culminates in his passion for ideas. He piques the curiosity of the reader as to how exactly one can manipulate past events.

He conjures up an eclectic, even eccentric image through the diverse collection of endeavours she has experienced in his young life and delivers these with humour. Quirky is what you might expect from an author of a dystopian novel, which inspires the reader to go check out his book.

Sankalp as his former suggests has pledged to waive off simplicity and embrace the embodiment of complex emotions into his write-ups ,this would be probably first time I am expressing my absolute love towards my love ,for more @improvkaar.

RETA winner and Guinness nominated writer Sankalp Mirani is back with this beauty . Bet , you will fall in love till the end.

DISCLAIMER

This book has been published with all reasonable efforts taken to make the material error-free after the consent of the author. No part of this book shall be used, reproduced in any manner whatsoever without written permission from the author, except in the case of brief quotations embodied in critical articles and reviews.

The Author of this book is solely responsible and liable for its content including but not limited to the views, representations, descriptions, statements, information, opinions and references.

The Content of this book shall not constitute or be construed or deemed to reflect the opinion or expression of the Publisher or Editor. Neither the Publisher nor Editor endorse or approve the Content of this book or guarantee the reliability, accuracy or completeness of the Content published herein and do not make any representations or warranties of any kind, express or implied, including but not limited to the implied warranties of merchantability, fitness for a particular purpose. The Publisher and Editor shall not be liable whatsoever for any errors, omissions, whether such errors or omissions result from negligence, accident, or any other cause or claims for loss or damages of any kind, including without limitation, indirect or consequential loss or damage arising out of use, inability to use, or about the reliability, accuracy or sufficiency of the information contained in this book.

ABOUT THE BOOK

Love isn't safe. And whoever you love will hurt you. It's part of the human experience. No one is perfect... people make mistakes. The secret is to focus on what they do right and decide what quirks you can live with. Set wide the window. Let me drink the day. I always thought that when people said, "love is not selfish," they were fooling themselves. But now I'm guided by the principle that it's okay to put aside what you feel for the welfare of another—for someone else's happiness—as long as you don't compromise yourself. Now I think there is no greater proof of love than that. I wish

Feelings had an On and Off button. That would make things easier for so many people. Because I know I have feelings for him, I know I'm fooling Myself by saying, "I'm falling in love with her," when the truth is that I'm Already in love. There's no turning back, even if admitting what I feel doesn't change anything. She doesn't feel the same way, so I have to swallow my Feelings and go on with my life as if nothing happened.

"I have loved the stars too fondly to be fearful Of the night."

No not really, if you just love chlorine for the smell I would be concerned, but if it has some sort of sentimental value to you then it's okay! As goes for the love....

Love

I may have not fallen head over heels ,

I may not called you but got the chills ,

I may hate your obsession for reels ,

But baby you gotta give me the feels.

I never get tired of you ,

Even if you talk toxic shit ,

I never vist the loo ,

You gonna brace your hoo-hoo ,

You gonna face the zoo ,

The burning tree embraces me ,

I am Angelino and a phoenix z ,

I like to live without any fee ,

But my bars are heavy like Bruce Lee ,

I love you passionately ,

I can kiss you ,

If you will , I may miss you ,

But we never met , but we had a meet ,

Everyday in our fuckhead heat ,

I love you mate , I love you bro ,

My words are less to describe ho-ho ,

We laugh , we slither , I am stupid you Peter , I love you feather , even I feel hots for your sister , you know my secrets you brother , you are the best xoxo clear ,

You don't fall or rise in love , you just get stuck.

STUCK IN LOVE

Old songs and old poems ,

Old Music and old sons ,

Old ones and golden sun's ,

Love is eternal peaceful bliss,

Glistening glossier glossery bitch ,

Hitch a hoop or hola a high ,

Baby you are my ,

You are one that never make me cry ,

I won't die livin' you lie ,

Comment up your vulgar bye,

You were harsh I know ,

Remember to be as cool as snow ,

Better than gibberish you glow ,

Unlike others you are matte ,

And that matters for that matter ,

Unlike others you are cute ,

And that's all its worth for ,

Babe I love you that you know ,

I made sacrifices to keep your ass in fire ,

And so I deserve a Xoxo,please don't negate ,I can't again wait and again go to bate , don't forget the three s of relationship- Serendipity,sex and success.

YOU

I fell in love lol

That too online lol

And that too with you lol

You broke my heart lol .

That too in quarantine lol

And you are smart lol

You will never get few lol

I Killed you pew pew lol

I fell in love online lol

Shraddha, **My paramour**

I may not have met you in real ,

But my heart's got you ,

What a person , alike personality ,

Hooked me as I was a teen ,

Blown absolutely as I looked ,

Your visage is cream of the life ,

For such smile how many strive ,

I loved you at first sight ,

You got my eyes even peeping night ,

I can't think anyone else possessing such legacy , c'mon you won my heart and Kapoor's disdcendeny , Animal care , human love ,half girl mine family adorer ,

A living goddess and a romcom crush ,soft hearted and rain-loving ,what you want more ,you adore the paramour ,

Amicable nature ,free spirit soul ,does what she says , not nays challenges she is here to stay , when she cries earth mourns ,.one actress that everyone are fan blind ,

Though a talent with the best smile and a aspiring figure , Shraddha actress of new world and mine.....first celeb crush

When love last ,my heart blasts ,

Life has long way to go unlike to casks ,

We have to express us do our tasks ,

We have breaths limited unlimited to last..

Hype is more than issue that hye ,

We get old eventually we die/dye ,

We have to laugh and smile at cry z,

Not to mention liable for styes ...

It gets hard and harder as goes dick ,

We have to choose seldom pick ,

We cannot cheat can't flick ,

Sometimes it's not just about licks....

I warn you therefore be careful early ,

Because it do complicate things get curly ,

Not much affirm about you getting surely ,

Not a flicker of birds that get ugly.....

You are one she should value ,

Not sticking balls with a super-glue ,

Unfolded truths lead nowhere herbrew ,

But Most careful while dealing her brew.....

King is back he claims his throne ,

No,the meaning changes in meantime crone, hard to fly get a drone ,

Heart gone is now hard gone.........

Forlorn I stranded amongst your standards, Like linked disease associated with back hurt, Love lived for few days with Googlie - moogle , But in the end was all struggle , Who will teach ya ? What not to do bro , I am like a sad crow , Who doesn't know where is the pot , Nor I smoke the coke, Thy say the late is cat , But what to do if heart broke . Like hot hamburgers , Like borboubon blue , As marine as it could be , With shells anew , Let death be served peacefully , Not as heartbreaks, hump the daylight ,

You ask how I am feeling,

I feel my cries ,I feel my lies,my soreful death eyes, all the ties to the mies to travel wrong way for miles;,

You say why I am feeling,

To **the quietest Quietus**, to the rafiq's baiters , to the layman's links ,to the cornea that blinks ,to the rover that snuffed ,to the ab-raham having lunch,

To the Croatian pubes and the tainted nubiles , to the hottest Sudan and spine chilling Chiles. To youthful yugenasia and pessimistic Palestine ,to ring Iraq and eleven two nine

You Qouth how I endure,

Pittfulfy pestering Pittsburgh Steelers,

Nefarious naked nude neutrophilic neurophiles, like a cat on hot tin roof , between billions but aloof,Hard heated heartbreaks hump ,I want to but I can't jump, tummy twisting tingling tickles, tickets, inferno purgatory are my home titles, like looking like liverbees Liverpool to the London lullabies ,I cross crossfields holding my crotch, cutting edges to be eminent Eminem, High hyped high guys, goons with dried galls ,can't turn a lesbian wet, thunder about thy balls, masseuse mocking at least jay bird , believe me you are a nerd, I am not the herd, my organ will be worldwide heard ,keep better quite you qualityless ass,think quadrice before you ask.

My Moaning Moon

Wtf is the world paused moon?

Why the night feels like noon?

Why doesn't it end soon

Wherever I see there is gloom

Foolish friends unlike you moon,

Unlike the lilies in which you bloom

Unlike bast**ds I would like to groom,

Why the feel is deadly in every room

Even though you come to see and vroom,I would like a
ride with you moon

To the moon and back

Amongst the stars,

Just me,my but and you moon,

I want to go in you to pursue peace

With this world between grease,

I would love to have a feast

In East while sun is sleeping,we will eating

With you moon just with you.....-

Hey girl , the way you swirl,

Can you make me fall of course you stand so tall,life is lies but you're beyond that I can see in your eyes, when I roll the dice,my heart freeze like an ice, I die to make your ties ,I love you girl, just beyond

This world , you don't mean the world, you are my universe, I want you in my every verse, in every way possible ,in every day plausible , without deniability without any pause any departure you are my artery you are my brochure , you are designed for me , designated for someone else, I Will love you till I cross ten hells ,even Angeles 'angles ring the bells to love you to the final knell. I will be sombre for you ,even I will be shattered apart ,I just want to be your one , the only one in your heart.

Friends of mine who want lumsum money ,

Friends of mine who want Rideout's funny ,

Friends of mine who want real love,

Who want business as white as dove.

I love them but a special one always prevails, the one on the lip as it hails,

I gotta go through rains, to absorb the stains, whatever be cost effective for bananas, I will prefer strawberries ,I love you lerrie ,till death's merry. I gotta get thrill in you , you are my Hebrew ,I love you girl till perdition knew, my sedition is true ,I make you new ,I love you too, I love you boo, you are my bee you are my Lee , you are the cure as my tea, I love you my bitch ,baddest of all, toddler for me. We started as friends we will always be, as our four asses like to knee , let's get high , let's get together for the bread and butter, to the fullest utter. I love you friend the first one to my rescue, the first one with whom I flew...

When will the one will be forgotten by this over mesmerized by the extravaganza of the life; When will one understand the real Value of death, when will one understand that you ain't nobody who got to strive, when will you understand fishes in pot love the outer rose bed.

I gotta say I am a Simpsone ,a bad one; I live life full of fuckers who want lumsum,I get to live life without any disease and full of symptoms, bad bitches and gruesome green tongue.

I stink bad when I wake up, I feel like sleeping when the day's up, I love to leave the death hub, and eat my piece of corpse claim to be dumb, I claim to be numb, I understand everything remaining stagnant in this bullish water of bullshit,I am to succumb, I am to succumb.

I die of cold, I die of old, in this world of sold and smittening gold, in italics or in bold, I am a simp for death, many stories untold and many to unfold. Many will scrolls, fools will roll and cry-babies troll.

People bring in expectations of being rich and then have palpation of being homeless

Why Can't A girl propose

What if he didn't propose ?, should he only tell it?

I wanna propose ? to him,

I wanna express my feelings, and love ? towards him,

There is no matter of shyness ? in it,

I'm delighted to tell him I Love Him ❤?,

And hear those 3 words of love in return?,

I Love You, Idiot ?❤,

Melting my heart like chocolate? into a sweet one?.

Anonymity is power

You were unknown to me once,

I don't by what miracle I got to know.

But you are the goddess of my heart,

To whom I pray and to whom I bow.

I never confessed you,

That I was in love with you.

But no one can't hide love for longer,

Like the clouds hide the firmament blue.

Time wipes away pain,

Changes stories.

But it hasn't got the power,

To wipe away your memories.

The tears in my eyes will dry up,

It is for sure.

But how I can forget you,

My love for you was pure.

I am not sad,

For you or your reply my sweetest person.

Its not you who made me sad ,

It was my own expectation.

I wont blame you my dear ,

Probably you were not in my destiny.

But I will surely ask sorry,

For mistakes if I committed any.

For you in my heart,

There is a book of my emotion.

But I am presenting you its summary,

In few words of affection.

You were the queen of my heart,

And you always will be.

And I feel it that in your life too,

You will never forget me.

Now I give a thought to it,

How did you in my life enter?

But I know for sure,

You made my life better.

I will never ask you,

For love in return.

Because I loved you,

I wasn't doing any business transaction.

May you be the winner of fame?

Happiness, peace and prosperity.

May everyone take your name,

With honour, respect and dignity.

Wherever you are,

Be satisfied and contended.

Say with these lines

My letter for you ended.

Friendship

Friends alike ,

Good or bad ,

Morons are sad ,

We do break bad ,

Live in survival ,

Do have battles ,

Not storage wars ,

Smart enough to Defy jiffy ,

Probst or enough frost ,

Love to have donuts once in a while ,

Friendship is alike , whether or you not like , Kill it or not , we are in a knot ,

Killing it every time , slaying it everyday ....

What more to say. This was how I described my feelings for you in few words. Before loving you I Worship you as a goddess with all the good and great virtues. Your hands are with some kind of magic

My dear; their creations please my eyes and have a soothing effect on my heart. I will not be there as

Your lover that is true but I will be always your greatest fan, no one in the universe can replace me in

That case. Anyways stay happy and blessed .Love you like always ......

The fine spring day with warm wind waves

I waited for you, under cherry blossoms shade...

My bambi eyes searching your sight,

Holding the umbrella you gave me last summer night...

Comforting my heart that you'll soon arrive,

Seeing no more hope of your visit in jive...

The foolish me still reminiscing the sweet memories of our good days

That we made in the last summer vacay...

I still believe you'll come back one day,

Give me reasons and perk me up away...

Honey can we end tie's on a good note and Clive,

My heart still doesn't believes that we parted away in shucking, jive...

Heart's pain it is the most unbearable pain.....

But I couldn't bear at all,

In this world I gain....

I know I m bold, strong and courageous.....

I know but you don't know I too have heart and worth for prestigious....

But how long I prove myself to everyone.....

I know all hearing and feel my pain but you too helpless like a empty gun.....

Who will secure me in the story of life?

Only you can my almighty please help me I'm walking on the knife....

If you leave my hand I'll fall in the falls...

I believe you completely than anyone else.....

You Know very well what I m asking in my prayer, give me soon......

Whatever I wish you fulfil,

But now I'm asking you a precious a boon....

How far I'll walk lonely over the broken bridge dear....

I can't! Leave me alone, time will answer you very clear........

Even on the **darkest of day**,

Hardship on journey has a stay.

You climb and you fall,

But it's not permanent after all.

It is said –

Dust if you must!

Here, your endeavour is your dust,

And your success is must.

Today you're belief is living like a mist of comfort without,

Tomorrow you'll live with your life devout.

Affliction is in everyone's path,

Aim on center isn't possible in everyone's dart.

Rather than losing hope or feeling despair,

Remember the elegant times of affection & care.

Truth of misfortune is indeed like a dusty rose,

A quill of every bliss which has now froze.

Not every moment brings a bad time,

So your fortune will itself make you climb.

Misshapenness & cheerfulness is kinda inborn,

But it isn't suggesting you to act forlorn.

Today is your bad day

But tomorrow maybe not!

Live like a bird,

Because life is short!

WHISPERING HEARTBEATS AT NIGHT

She heard people saying that when someone misses a person at night,

That person will be insomniac,

Because their soul want to unite under the moonlight,

Experiencing the cool breeze.

She was in deep thought,

Cuddling her teddy bear,

Wondering who would miss her at that time,

Sacrificing his sleep.

She was missing the long late night telephonic conversation,

She was reading the WhatsApp chats again and again,

She was hoping to get a text from him,

As she saw him online.

Her heartbeats whispered to text him,

Her fingers automatically typed “I miss you”,

Suddenly she realized he was no more online,

Her mind asked her to press backspace to delete her text.

Her eyes were filled with tears,

Which were rolling down her cheeks?

Wetting her soft pillow,

Making her heart to throb.

Her heartbeats were murmuring,

Pleading her to stop hurting them,

By not thinking about the old days,

Asking her to move on for their sake.

Suddenly sunrays entered her room,

And touched her delicate cheeks,

She realized that again one more sleepless night was
added to her life,

She wiped her tears and smiled to welcome the new day

Falling into melancholy darkness,

Sweeping off all the positive thoughts,

Stripping to your bare self,

Engulfed in the self-consuming sorrow.

Need a hand to be held onto and saved,

But feel too afraid to ask,

Have soaked your body and soul,

In this "I'm fine" mask.

It has already pained and hurt so much,

That now all you feel is numbness,

Want to emerge out of it like a star,

But it will forever leave a scar.

Even if the grief has consumed you all,

It's okay,

It's okay because you know,

You'll rise

Like a winter bear from its hibernation,

Like a phoenix

From it's ashes

Trust me,

It will be fine,

Pick yourself, hold yourself, and face yourself,

You deserve to feel better.

Don't live in frail pieces,

It will take time,

But you'll heal just fine,

You yourself are enough to heal your crumbled soul.

When there is no light,

Shine, brighten and enlighten yourself,

You've seen your lowest and

Faced yourself without telling anyone else.

Be your own hope,

Be your own sun,

And always remember,

It's okay to be you!!

OUR CLANDESTINE

Happiness radiated by your persona,

With a smile plastered on your face,

What everyone sees is your corona,

And your fake "grace"

Should always be giggling on god-knows-what,

With misery kept miles away,

No signs of your bruised soul,

No signs of your SELF, that is crushed

That's how the world expects you to be,

Like a fable of Utopia,

Like "the happy prince",

Where all sorrow is forbidden

We all know we are broken,

We all know we are damaged,

Some are ruptured beyond repair,

Some just need a hand to hold on to

I should be happy,

Even though I'm sad,

I'm supposed to be joyous,

Even when I'm mad

This is how the world works,

No one wants to see the real YOU,

All want to see the mask,

That smiles and acts like a better you

No one wants to see the ugly us,

The broken us,

All everyone wants to see is,

Our clandestine.

Daisies never bloom

We both were drowning,

But you held onto me.

You became my anchor even in my wildest dreams,

The blue sky roared

But you were my calm.

I wish to be the same,

When my daisies were unharmed.

The spring came and flowers bloomed,

But my daisies were still waiting in the gloom,

I think we both were trying to hold our breathe,

Under the deep waves of life,

With guilt and regret.

A hand saved me then,

Yet, I was dropped from the moon.

Now the blue sky is gone,

And the daisies never bloom,

It is 8 in the morning hate in the morning,

However, I am grey.

I wait for the showers,

I wait for the sunlight,

But I am still grey.

When will the sky glow?

When will the rain wash me clean?

When will the light sparkle?

Is this me?

Or am I in a dream?

You said the flowers bloom in spring

So why does my daisies never bloom?

Our Promise....

Hidden world in you make my fear to hide,

Broken pieces of burden tears reflects our happiness,

Caring and consoling is your character,

But now cumulated the cumbrance of responsibility cubit and make you a promise..

Fiddle feud between our hearts and

Flare of feat raises a hope of flit.

I explored the world in you over your heart,

That made me to accept the promise

Which never not to break..

I'm sturdy and stun like a strut and

Now make your promise come again

To revive me... To complete me....!!

Immortal magic...

My musical medicine for mediocre dream,

Mesmerizing Mortifies muted my mornstream..

Misprinted moments owing to our happy dream,

Misplayed mistakes miserable to our happy frame..

Many magical moments making me happy,

For being without you reminds me to feel pity myself....

Muted chat waiting for a sound and

Broken heart asking me to fill in your bond!!!

FARE WELL

A memory which lasts with time

A memory always lasts till the lift time

You can't take my memory always

With all the things that happen with me

And many more to say

I know the days will be though ahead

And time will take it all I know

Don't have words to evened out and show

But I just want to tell you

That my dear I will surely miss you !

Life is a dangerous game of emotions.

Feels like engraving through Motions.

Everything matters with power of thoughts.

Desires are like deepest classic notes.

Feelings are like gamble.

Mind stuck in vary of trouble.

Tears melting day by day.

Saturday turning as sad day.

If you're establish self as emotional person.

You have to face people's different version.

You have to boil as food like fame

Shuffling yourself in this toughest game.

Loving yourself is the key to a happy life. When you love all that you are, unconditionally, life reflects That back to you. When you learn to love yourself, fully, you create a happy, loving environment to Flourish in. When we lose sight of what's most important—loving self—we lose sight of our goals and dreams and being happy and healthy. Ultimately, to live a fulfilling life, first and foremost, requires that

You love all that you are and trust that life loves you in return.

Love is the core of who you innately are. It's highly important to practice loving yourself day to day Because it will bring you true and everlasting happiness, inner peace and will improve your heath and Wellness. How you speak to yourself is how your feel about yourself deep within, and reflects The past is over, let it go. Forgive and then forget. Allow the power of God to heal your heart and soul by trusting in Him and feeling His pure love for you. You are a cherished daughter of a loving Heavenly father who only wants the very best for you. You are divinely watched over and guided continually—

Trust in Him.

As you come to love yourself more fully do so with gratitude. Love your faults and look for the best in Your body. As you move forward in reaching your goals support yourself love by honouring your body. Make goals to eat healthier and exercise regularly. Your body is your temple—treats it as such. And in so Doing, your love will expand, you will become more passionate about life, you'll be able to think better, And you'll be happier and healthier.

Dearest duke,

You are my best friend, am too lucky to have you in my life that I can't even express in words.

Nothing makes me more happier when you are around .You are such a person in this whole world who Hears me all time leaving all that is behind only for my tears that you love to erase and hide. Each and Every time I am better because of you. I cannot stop thinking about you. My love for you is unconditional and eternal.

Your honesty, generosity, kindness and loyalty !

You're one of the kindest people I've ever been lucky enough to know. You're a great listener.

Your strength inspires me. You have the best laugh. You're a blessing to me and my strength. I cherish you, and I cherish our friendship. It means so much to know you're on my side. Thank you for all the

Times you've been there for me when I needed you the most to share everything. Thanks for putting up with me.

Your friendship means so much.

You'll always be one of my very favourite people.

The saddest part is,

That I know I'll be okay,

But still everything is awful,

I know that there are some people who love me, But still, I feel unloved,

I know that doing the things I love will make me feel better,

But I don't know why all of them do nothing like that,

I want to be well,

But I also know that I can't survive until there.

THE FEELING OF PAIN INSIDE.

There is a feeling of being so vulnerable

To all the pain that bears in my heart, I don't know where my way I never made a perfect start is Things have changed for me

There is nothing left to see

I think there was never a moment

When I got to enjoy my glee

I have strived hard through the pain

I have suffered all in the vain

Happiness has a role to play in life

Its just sadness which

I have seen Struggling for a moment to smile

All the while in time....

Waiting is a root of love

Men and women are lovers,

Dreamily Coming around love flowers,

Women are flowery trees,

Men are hungry bees.

Pain is the healthy water to make love grow,

Tears are like blood when they flow,

Hearts squeeze dreams like rain,

Longing for someone is great pain.

Waiting for someone is a root,

To make love sprout,

Slowly and steadily like the moon,

When it does brightly burn.

Within closed eyes, someone dances,

In sleep, dreams create more chances,

To recollect our favourite face,

In a dreamy and fast pace.

THE SHINING FIRE INSIDE OF ME

I have been hurt,

Trampled and insulted,

And I cried so many times.

I became angry and swore to myself,

That I would never forgive,

Those who oppressed me.

But they say,

Promises are meant to be broken,

And I have proved it to be true.

Because, eventually,

I'm still able to forgive,

People who have hurt me.

Whatever I do,

My heart softens and melts like jelly.

The fire of God that burns within me,

Is so strong, it's dazzling,

And truly powerful!

I could do nothing to resist,

The shining fire inside of me.

For love?

I have but a heart

Here it's in my hands

I give it to you

And know it's not much

For your unconditional love

For longing?

I have but a soul

I took it out of my body

To dwell within you

Words?

I know but three words

That I whisper to you

With all my heart and soul:

I love you

Open your eyes

Put on a fake smile and say you're okay

Show pain

I know it feels like an hour in the rain

Sitting alone , acting all strange

And people are like , that dude's insane

Let me tell you one thing and it'll be okay

Your mind is a powerful place

Don't let it control you with a powerful pace

It's gonna tell you that you're fine

But you know you're not

So don't even try

This life is full of pain , there's no need to cry

Hold on , sit back tight

Don't tell yourself , hell , its gonna be alright

Put on a damn smile and take flight

Go follow that bright light

Fly and enjoy the magical ride

I haven't seen more beautiful

Than the language of the eyes

They talk, cry, rejoice and smile

They appreciate, like, and madly fall in love

Without uttering a single word

The eyes are the mirrors

Of our hearts and souls

Their language is one

Of the most eloquent

It conveys a full speech without words

It expresses all feelings without a touch

It is the language of silence in the sea of words

It is the language that dives into the depths of feelings

Around The Clock

Time will tell,

Is a tale.

The clock ticks every second,

But only wisdom can tell when it is time.

Life is a rat race against time,

A game of flashing seconds,

You cannot rewind the clock,

So you've got to keep up the pace.

Decisions determine your speed against time,

Distance is a matter of chance,

Direction's a matter of choice,

If you can't outrun time,

You'll run out of time.

Ignorance corrodes time,

Eternity is on the other side of time,

Where time determines timelessness,

Outside time, account for time.

You can't buy time,

So don't kill time.

You'll win this race,

Only if you can keep time!

"Respond in Kind"

The break of day begins with dawn.

The darkness of the night is gone.

Time continues on and on.

To life's conditions, we respond!

We have got an inside track.

There's someone there who's got your back!

To have the faith to trust your gut,

Is not a matter of blind luck!

You must play an active role

To make progress towards your goal.

The God inside will build your soul.

Let Him control your mind's console!

Decide right now your inner light

Will guide your steps when life's a fight!

Enlightenment within is where

The light begins! Become aware!

Today my goal is going to be

To find best ways for You and me

To help some other folks be free

And not live life upon their knees!

When you look inside you find

The spark inside you is Divine!

Let It plot your inncr course

And It will lead you to Its source!

Thank You to the God within.

I give thanks for where I've been!

For even when life seems a fight,

Peace is spread by inner light!

In this life you will lose

Only those worth losing

Whoever loves and respects you

Will find a thousand reasons to stay

Mind is slippery

Mind is sometimes slippery,

When I have unwanted worry,

About what happened before,

Like an empty seashore.

Thoughts bloom and wither,

Bad habits haven't stopped either,

Nothing changes when I am in sorrow,

Seriously thinking about tomorrow.

No sun in my sky,

Dreamily my thoughts fly,

Like the broken wings of a bird,

When I feel sad.

Tears, eyes spill,

Like the clouds on the hill,

No hopeful plants in growth,

When my heart is like the barren earth.

My love,

I need you to live

You touch my soul

You water my heart

I breathe your love

Day and night

Our relation is a source

Of comfort and peace of mind

Of unconditional love

Of true friendship

You love me as I am

With all my flaws and qualities

With all my darkness and light

You embrace me

With all your tenderness

My heart was born to love you

My mind was created to understand you

And my soul to worship you

To worship your devotional love

To thank the Divine for having you

My special loving soulmate

May our love get us closer

May our mutual dedication and sacrifice

Lead us to the temple within our soul

Where our love is sanctified forevermore

My love,

I met you by coincidence

Then I loved you

Then I became addicted to you

And I swore loving no one but you

For you conquered all my heart

If they ask me about my happiness

I'll tell them your name

My sweet loving soulmate

And if they ask me about my wish

I'll tell them to be close to you

And If they ask me about the best day of my life

I'll tell them that I registered my birthday

The day I met you

And before that date...

I don't even remember what I lived

My days without you

Are lifeless, colourless and dull

My days without you

Are like a rose with ripped petals

Or a bird with broken wings

My days without you

Are like an oak tree searching

For a land for its roots

If you can't find the half that suits you

Beware from accepting any other half

Because your misery will start from here

When you accept the one who doesn't suit you

TENDERNESS

My love

Let's climb the ray of light

Travel with the breeze...

Let's perfume the air with the breath of our love

Exhaust dreams with our hopes

Paint butterflies' wings with the colours of our longing...

Let's go with the sun as it sets

And come back with it as it rises

So we're no longer separated by death

Nor set apart by age or sleep!

O love of my soul!...

Let our love

Fill the space

Draw on the haze of the skies

Engrave on the walls of the temples

Write on the sands of the beaches

And on the surface of the seas

An eternal love lesson

Played by two lovers

Or rather by all lovers

On the stage of life...

Let's travel in the clouds

Fly with the falcons

Draw lines from the ether

The beauty of our love...

Don't take your hand away from mine

Let the heat of your love run through my veins

Infiltrate my soul

And remain there as an eternal sun,

To keep me warm for generations...

Don't take your eyes off mine

Your eyes are the sea of my happiness

In which my soul sails towards its horizon

Towards its wisdom

Towards its divinity

In the sphere of your eternal love

Keep me close to you

So I hear the sound of your breath

A symphony of eternal love

The rhythm of a completed existence

In which life is exalted with its firstborn son

And my self is exalted with its only lover!

Let's take a walk at night

To illuminate it with a ray of hope

To teach the oyster its longing for the pearl

And the boat its love for the sail!

Let's walk and don't stop

The paths of love are drawn by our footprints

Landmarks are set by our work

Detours are drawn by our parting

And endings are renewed by our reunion!

Oh love of love!

Let's go towards our horizon

Quench our thirst from the dew of tenderness

Nourish ourselves from the fragrance of heavens

For your love within my heart became my path outside time

My love,

I feel exalted

Whenever your spectrum

And a breeze from your heart

Come knocking on my heart's doors

Wandering around my gardens

Waking up my soul from its slumber

Pulling me towards a dream

That leads to a beautiful destiny

And I reply to you with the whispers of my soul

With the burning sighs within my heart

With the longing of my senses

And with your love that flows through my veins

Tell me that you love me as I do

That the longing is burning your heart too

That my moon is illuminating your nights

And that my stars are orating your skies

If my love is a sin, then forgive me

But may I ask you to return my soul to my body?

For she left me to embrace your love

Swearing that she'll never ever come back to me

For she found in you her everlasting homeland

Oh my sweet loving soulmate

How I love you!

SERENITY

Let's melt, my love, the snow of the past

Warm the days with the heat of our longing

Crown the peaks with the glow of our pursuit

Adorn hearts with the colour of our love...

Let's walk and don't stop

Rise to the mountains highs

So peaks learn pride from us

And then go down the slopes

To teach slopes the secret of humility and ambition

Let's travel the far seas

To teach the sea the dream of reunion,

The secret of the sea merging with horizons

And the secret of the sea meeting the shores...

Let's fly in the fresh air

To teach eagles the love of highs

And birds the beauty of tweeting....

Let's go for a walk in the fields of nature

To teach roses the softness of tenderness

And scents the secret of spreading...

Let's bless all paths

With the footsteps of love

The infinite love that was born within us

And in which we will be born

Through an eternal unity!

Let's sip the nectar of flowers

Drink the wine of nature

So the earth is exalted by the breath of our love...

Let's sip the dew of days

So time learns faithfulness from our promise

And ages are quenched by our loyalty!

Let's write on the temples' walls the wisdom of love

The legend of two lovers:

Separated by the word at first

United by the meaning of the word in the end!

Let's play on the strings of hearts

Seven symphonies

Immortalized by life as a memory

Sung by every mouth

Every mother's whispering to her new-born

In every silent night

Until silence falls asleep

The night resting from its journey

And voices in the throats become silent

Remains only one voice

Whispering 3 words

Echoed through the depths of silence

And heard by every creature:

I love you!

Disputes are the best test

For love and friendship

Some argue with you

Yet their feelings towards you

Stay deep, honest and true

And your relationship is unaffected

Others argue with you

And though your relationship ended

They still respect you

And preserve your dignity

And others argue with you

Destroying everything

That ever existed with you

The true colour of love

And the real motives of the relation

Are only revealed by the major

Ordeals that hit the relationship

And this proves the strength

And resistance of the relation

Facing the storms of life

Nobody changes with time

It is just the masks that fall

WHEN I KISS YOU.

Oh! My love,

I am always sure it is you I love,

I am always certain it is you I want to live with,

I am always assured it is you I want to risk all with,

Even when everything around me is unsure,

Even when I am exhausted from pursuing my dreams,

Even when I am discouraged to fight for my rights,

Even when I am confused on the path to follow,

My courage, confidence, clarity, and certainty are assured,

When I kiss you.

Life is full of beautiful moments

And these moments aren't related

Where you are

But with whom you are

Any place becomes paradise

When we're with the one

We appreciate and love

And a palace may turn to a prison

When love and affection are absent

Roses, an expression beyond love

Symbolic to the emotion of love,

An expression of one's pure passion,

Roses stem feelings to rise above,

Elating the heartbeats in just a fraction.

Celebrating love with its alluring fragrance,

Elevating emotions to that pinnacle of sensuality,

Roses whisper those unsaid words in silence,

Pulsating desires, irrespective of sexuality.

Comforting the distressed with its striking colour,

Calming the pain, adding to life that vibrance,

Roses soothe sorrows with their distinct savour,

Reviving hope, bringing back that endurance.

Cheering up the ailing with a spirit of revival,

Restoring positivity for that speedy recovery,

Roses empower healing, beyond what's medical,

Bringing life back, to its normal journey.

Being dead itself, extending varied expressions,

From adoration, affirmation, to acceptance and affection,

Roses subtly, tie in various connections,

Reflecting emotions, in harmonious perfection.

Awaking

When I wake for you

From the earth beneath

Trust me love

I am for you

Forlorn is the dream

But it is beautiful

I reside in you

Is that not enough?

The beam of you

I walk on honey

Is that not enough?

To radiate you

Silence of darkness

When you illumine

The snowflakes house

Ignite the moon

Abandoned in the valley

Lore of love for all

When will we shape

The truth inside

For a long time

I've been alone

Long time

That I do not care about anyone

But when you said "hello"

My heart beats faster

And I can't speak

Not a single word

Comes out into my mouth

As day goes by

I fell in love with you

But I know it's too early

To admit what I feel for you

I know we love each other

But I'm afraid to fall in love again

Love or don't love

But only one word

I want to hear from you

Just one word

For me to say the magic word

If you love me

Don't hesitate to say it

'Coz my heart just whispered

That I love you too

Love is a secret

Unspoken words are a lot

Burning in my trembling heart,

Love is what,

To make life great.

Words are not important,

When love comes to live like a tenant,

In other heart like a secret,

With long and unforgettable regret.

It's so simple to love everyone,

With fake love and fun,

But pure love is like gin,

To make every heart to win.

My love,

I often wondered...

How can you fill my soul with so much love?

How can you make me feel reborn anew?

How can you be my sunshine in winter?

How can you be my rainbow in the storm?

How can you turn my heart from a desert

To a paradise garden?

Then I recalled that...

Soulmates' love is omnipresent

Beyond time and space

They share the same soul imprint

They share the same heart root

They're forever connected

By an invisible thread

So I understood that...

You've been living within my heart all along

As our hearts share the same pulse

Hence, true love filled with faithfulness

Loyalty, devotion and dedication

Will break all barriers between us

And the two halves of our souls

Can unite back as one forevermore ❤??

I'd like one day to meet myself

Shake my hand

Invite myself for a cup of coffee

Exchange with her conversations

And smiles...

Then say to her:

It was a great pleasure meeting you

Your goodness is a distinctive quality

It's not a stupid flaw

How I wish one day

To become my own friend!!

My Love,

I meet you in my soul

I indulge from your embrace

I see you in my heart

And can't stop looking at your face

I reach out to you in my thought

I feed my soul from your longing

I breathe you in my ethereal body

And wear your love wherever I go

I don't have to explain myself to you

You read me like an open book

I trust you'll be with me when angels leave

Your love is so true and real

You don't need to doubt my love

I wrote my heart in your name

You'll always be my shelter

My soul is yours forever

INTIMATE LOVE.

I just want to be intimate with you,

As my hands get knitted with your hands,

As my body melts into your body,

As my thought agrees with your thought,

As my mind gets united with your mind,

And my spirit becomes one with your spirit,

So that when I look into you,

I see me in you,

And when you look into me,

You see me in you,

So that we become intimately in love.

YOUR EVERYTHING MATTERS TO ME THE MOST

Oh dear –

As –

You are my bright dawn

You are my sunshine..

You are my loving

Addiction

You are my Valentine ..

You are my endless horizon

You are my skyline..

You are my cosy nest

You are my coastline..

That's why –

Your everything matters to me

Matters to me the most..

Be it –

Your dew or your mist

Your nectar or your wine ..

Your destiny or your goal

Your life or your lifeline..

Your sorrow or your peace

Your will or your wish..

Your joy or your bliss

Your time or your timeline..

Knowingly or unknowingly

By fault or by design.

Being my first date

Being my first crush..

Being my first illusion

Being my cloud nine..

OH MY VALENTINE

Oh my dear

Oh my Valentine

Leave your present

Leave your past..

Leave your first

And leave your last..

Hope and desire

Love and admire

And

Leave your footmark's

Leave your footprints..

In my feathers

In my wings..

In my life

In my lifeline..

In my soul

And its timeline ..

In my arteries

In my veins..

In my memories

And in its lanes..

Without fail

Without miss..

To convey your goodwill

And to convert your wish..

Clearly and directly

Certainly and earnestly..

Definitely and absolutely

Totally abs completely..

I once had a star.

Born of energy acted out between us.

As we expressed to each other, the heavenly hell a man may cause a woman, or woman a man.....

A brilliance awoke with light in a sea of black.

So small yet so bright.

We would observe with our instruments the development of our golden son.

As the rays of light burned, their growing day and night.

And we became attached to this spark of life inside us, as we trek a cosmos of emptiness.

Till one day, the little giant burned to bright to hold in the flesh.

So with leaking womb shaking hands and expressing eyes we opened ourselves. And let go.

The little son floated away. Higher and higher. And when you look up, you see him bright in the night to this day.

But....Never to hold his warmth to my chest, feel his heart beat and his sweet breath.

But what's mine is mine, even if it's unknown. And his twinkle is the mark of my own. Perhaps one day, the light from my star may reveal me.

Brighten the darkness in which I wait for that day of fate.

His glow will shine through time.

Till released from the heavens grasp, with streaking trails marking his course back to me.

So I might be there to catch him in a father's embrace or get bonked in the head by him with my surprise, but with her grace.

Till that day, I wait for him every night. Eyes in the skies.

Waiting for the day I may call what's mine, mine. And tell him I've caught him before, when he was born. So watching him go away was the hardest experience I've had to this day. If he can forgive me, for what I haven't done, and what I have. It will make him a better man than I. So, be better than me, my son. Make the best of your years to come.

My love,

I believe,

We are made to love each other

Our hearts are a perfect match

You've got my heart's missing pulse

And I have yours

I believe,

We are soulmates

We are the two halves of the same soul

We have the same soul imprint

You're my man, I'm your woman

I believe,

The universe conspires for true lovers to meet

For our destiny is to return as one soul

To walk as pilgrims on the sacred path of unconditional love

Where compromise and sacrifice are trifles

Where loyalty, safety and mercy are tangible

I believe,

We didn't reunite by coincidence

May God bring us closer forever

For without your love, I cannot live

Only you love me as you love yourself

Only you feel me though distance apart

Only you read my silence

Only you see your soul through mine

Only you love me unconditionally just as I am

I believe,

I want to be with you... only you... for eternity

EMBRACE

Oh my love

Why were you separated from me

Why did your name hide itself from my tongue...

Why did your existence leave my faith?!

Despair almost took possession of my soul

Fear nearly captured my hope,

Fear that you don’t come back

That you forget the most sacred promises!

Where were you my love

Did the face of the moon make you forget my face

Or the blow of the wind made you forget my voice!..

Did a new aim distract you from my love?

Let me love it too

Your love is my love

Your heart is my heart

And your happiness is my happiness!

Who kept you away from your happiness?

Is it a flying eagle in space

Or a passing meteor in the sky

Is it a scent you followed to the farthest places

Or an ambition pulled you towards glories?!

But life doesn’t differentiate between its two halves

Their parting from one another is the ultimate duality

Their union is the pinnacle of unity

The sanctity of love!

Let's unite

Let's revive the vows we made

Let's go back to the perfection we built

Come back to the present

And let the past burn its memory!

My love

As longing lasted too long

Let's travel to the world of dreams

Dreams we fulfil together

In the world of completed love,

The world of great happiness!

Come to me my love

Leave the sea of forgetfulness behind you

With the boat of separation

And the pain of parting...

Come back to your world

To my world

That was devoided of life

Even from beings

There was nothing but the ghost of waiting

And the illusion of dying

Till you came back...

Illusions were dissipated

Life moved in the wombs

And dreams were awakened

Stay with me

With yourself

In the kingdom of passion!

The Ghost of You

The man I knew is dead and gone,

Sweet memories still linger on.

My heart has broken right in two,

I'll always love the ghost of you.

Fire felt long ago has passed,

Romantic feelings failed to last.

Long for heated passion I do,

I'll always need the ghost of you.

Which path might we each choose,

No matter what, both stand to lose.

Wounded spirits cry without a clue,

I'll always miss the ghost of you.

I hunger for the gentle, tender touch,

Of he who once needed me so much.

Warm kisses freely given, now feel blue,

I'll always want the ghost of you.

Hope for the future we both lack,

Knowing there's no turning back,

Cold sorrow grows inside its true,

I'll always mourn the ghost of you.

Sometimes a partner's personality can change drastically after many years of togetherness. It feels as if that person died, replaced by an unfamiliar disposition.

BROKEN THOUGHTS

THE ROAD TO GOD

Man has always been worshipping God since the stone age. It is because man's inner chemistry of body and soul demands it. We are all trying to find God in our own ways.

Sometimes in the search of God, we take the wrong turn ending at the road of chaos. The worst thing is that man starts creating his own manifested Gods. The search of God should take you to the path of wisdom and enlightenment. It will surely free you from all the fears of the unknown. The true search will make you the believer of the unseen.

It will turn you into a new "fearless you". You will be free and brave enough to think to ponder to move against herd psychology.

The love and wish to see and meet God will make you the ultimate interdimensional being. A being or a lover free of space and time.

True wisdom will never allow you to make multiple Gods of needs. These Gods of money and power will only make you more fragile and fearful. The belief in the true God will simply make you invincible.

NIGHT CONVERSATION

My sweetheart, where have you been?

Whenever the sun sets

Whenever the night gets darker

Whenever mountains rise

Whenever two lovers meet

I called you...

Where have you been my love

In which age

In which castle?

In which era?!

Why did life separate us

Why did you leave my world

Why did you confine yourself in past memories

And imprisoned the future within the vividness of my self?

Let me dry your tears

Their drops burn my ribs

Hurt my soul

And inflame my wounds...

Forgo the sadness of the past

Throw away fear and pain

And the memory of a storm

Sail in the sea of forgetfulness

And forget the separation!

Let the past mourn its ashes

Take off your sad look

And let's celebrate the reunion,

A reunion that blesses the eternity of our souls!

Promise me my endless love

Promise that you won't leave me anymore

Let not a dream or sleep separate us

Without you

My soul is cold and barren

My heart beats an illusion

The blood in my veins runs a mirage!

I thought you were lost within myself

And started looking for you tirelessly!

Even my depths were devoid

Of echo

Of scope

Of silence...

Devoid except

Of your memory

Of your confidences' perfume

Of your smile sparkle

And of my longing for you...

Stay close to me

As the flame remains by the lamp

As the foam remains by the waves

And as the scent of freedom remains by the forests...

Friendship

Friendship is not about someone you are fooling It's about understanding and never controlling Friendship always comes with a friendly embrace

It will Friendship hurts sometimes when it gives us the truth But can be beneficial when trying to get through Friendship raises us up when we hit rock bottom True friends will be recognized by the ones who have got 'em Friendship is never judging it will always offer control

always be honest and never two faced

Respect for one another never acting like a fool Friendship is always there when we're on our last leg

There to pull us through never asking us to beg

Friendship is never selfish never being one sided It is tolerant unconditional making sure we are guided

When finding a true friend make sure it lasts forever To be there for one another throughout life's endeavour...

We used to love now we don't

we were no ordinary lovers we loved out loud never undercover

we used to sit in each other's face and smother the other with an abundance of love and in doing so we found great comfort we used to laugh at your brother he cracked jokes all during supper he was your role model that was easy for me to discover

we used to disagree about your mother because i was not from her same southern in the beginning you didn't care we were lovers, we used to be designed for one another I'll never forget that summer

we used to love now we don't

- Now we are complete strangers again

Go

Leave the past, stay with me

Let's continue the journey of life together

I didn't make a single step without you

And my soul has vowed silence, until I find you!

Come on, let's go to our eternal paradise

Where there is no separation after today!

Leave them without regret

There is better, kinder people

Cherish your heart

Don't be satisfied with little

You deserve someone who chooses you

Who values your presence in their life

Rather than drains life out of you

And leaves you in a state of confusion

You need loving and tender hearts

Not toxicity and pain

As soon as you feel hurt, leave

You're in the wrong place!

And if you ever have to choose

Between being loved

And being respected

Always choose respect

For love without respect

Is ephemeral

Whereas mutual respect

Can change into a lasting

Love relation

I really did it to myself this time i let someone in and they are a two faced ass bitch who only needs you for so long and then when they got what they wanted they dont need you anymore and it kills me to open up to people anyways so the people i do

Open up to i trust with my life but then people wanna come and take that trust that i have built up and destroy it and it breaks me more and more i knee i should have just kept telling my mom but i thought that if i could just trust i would get

Further no i just fell deeper into my lil hole that i dug myself and when i came a close to the light the person i thought cared pushed me right back into it so the next time someone asks me if im ok just dont ok im not going to tell you because i

Have opened up to a few people and they have tour me apart and you know it will be the u think will have your back forever and they really dont they just want you until they have got what they needed and then they could give to shits about your

Stupid dumb life and u really thought that one person out of all people wouldn't leave well moral of the story dont trust its worse then love

Melting love

Melting in you like the snow's hue

Darling, I love you

Is the intoxication for you

Calm me for you

Your lips touch me

Like the ether inn

Many times I break

In the bosom deep

The water-filled earthen pot

Carry I all the way

You love the fancy flowers

Making me sit that way

Love in your eyes

Is my heaven guy

You the mystic vibe

Where I reside

When you flower my braid

I feel the angel inside

In these rustic hands

Your love survive

So Unjust!!!

It has become so shirty,

So Unjust that some lose their being,

It's so dark rather not easy at all,

The world is nobody's friend.

Every sunrise carries a burden,

Of it is unbearable,

But we live up to the circumstance,

Just yesterday we laughed,

But today we wonder,

If ever the wheel would spin back,

For some of us wronged,

And the blame it's no use.

Come free me,

Come free the world,

For the friends are the enemies,

The enemies that step aside for your downfall.

The mutual feel wouldn't be shaken,

As the believe is in that which doesn't last,

Only if pain is inside,

The outrageous mind roams around,

Like the bees to the flowers seeks the hope of change.

Change that will cure those sorrows,

To be a winner once again,

The fighter who never gives up,

The soldier whom made it at all times.

Regardless of the fate,

Once again the feel remain mutual,

As the heart prays for change,

And still hopes everything shall be how it should.

This poem is dedicated to my dearest ... we're together

In the hush the quiet the silence the stillness

In less than a whisper

In the slowly falling leaf

Sometimes

In the slight glimmer

The translucent light

The shade

I am aware.

Sometimes

I feel

In the boy

Buried for years

Inside me

In the heart

There is

God.

Touching me softly.

A gentle caress

A warmth

The giving

The surrender.

All here

Is love.

I think it's incredibly guilt inducing to talk about the same issue to friends because every time you bring it up, you question yourself as to whether it's really okay speaking about it when you did so just a few hours ago? Do they consider me close enough to open up to or is it just one sided and I'm the weird one? Will I lose this friendship because of not being able to get over a low that seems never ending and they'd just had enough of the negativity? Every time I speak about my lows these days, I feel guilty, even though the people around me have been kind enough to listen. I wish I could occupy the spaces they offer with happier thoughts so it would be easier to be around me, but I feel guilty for not being able to.

In a similar stride, I think I'm also very grateful for the ones who listen to me rant on what is now almost a daily basis. It's weird to think I have people care about me at times, given I often feel I do not deserve it. It's a rather new place to be for me where I'm often torn between guilt and gratitude in most of my conversations. All said, I am truly appreciative of the newer spaces that have been accepting of me and made me feel at ease amidst a duress.

Dirty Love

May a muse whisper to your‘ Sexy Talk dirty secrets, little pretty dove Dream to understand, dear You are the one; In a mind of dirty thoughts

I can envision a body, perfect picture Every way of making, lustful love In that smile don’t pretend, dear You crave the height of pleasure; In the moments that will come

Belong mine, in the luxury of moaning None so far, beyond the Golden Gates In a manner to feed upon emotion Then shall begin once my pretty learns to beg

Now, a lady entranced in bedroom pleasure As she drapes her lovely arms Making love until the light of morning Shall be deflowered; In the midst of, Dirty duress.

My love,

You fill my heart with

Tenderness

Happiness

Faithfulness

You taught me

Unconditional love

Hope and faith

Gratitude grace

Your love is divine

Hard to define

Soulful, beautiful

Deep and just as I need

Your love touches my soul

Heals my wounds

Empowers my will

To climb the highest hill

How great it would be

To celebrate you and me

Someday by the sea

Our soulful love endlessly

My Love,

Your tender heart is my world

With you I feel free like a bird

Spinning in the air high

Resting on a cloud in the sky

Your tenderness fills my heart with love

With safety, with the purity of a dove

Our love builds bridges in the sky

Where we meet each night, just you and I

My soul is full of longing

My heart to yours belongs

So let it be...

Let the power of our love

Transcend all the odds

As soulmates...

Our bond is sacred

Our love is fated

You're my tender half

I'm to you related

The earth may go in dismay

The sun may fade away

Yet our soulful bond

Will forever stay strong

Life Taught Me

? Your days won't come back

Do what makes you happy

? Don't be sad

No one will feel you

Except your health

? Set personal goals

And strive to achieve them

Don't give all your time to others

You are worthy of love and care too

? Before you get too attached to anyone

Be prepared for their absence

? Ignore anything

That steals your joy

Live free

? Seek approval and validation

From God and your conscience

Never from people!

? Walk away from anyone

Who doesn't value your presence in their life

Dignity is above love and friendship

Dignity is your second soul

Never lose it!

? Never blame someone

Who deliberately do things to hurt you

Who belittles your sadness

Withdrawing from their life silently

Saves your dignity

? Amid the various options

Always choose yourself

? Be picky in your battles

You don’t need to attend every

Argument you’re invited to

Sometimes staying calm

And silent are the best answer

? As you don’t accept dirt on your clothes

Hate, anger, fear and resentment

Are spots of dirt in your heart

Put all your worries in God’s Hands

For the love of God NEVER fails

? No one deserves the chance

To deserve you twice

? Always smile ?

For in the end

All will pass!

Thank you so much

For the love and care

That you delivered

In my entire life

You are the only one

That have put a smile and happiness

Without asking anything in return

In our true love

There is nothing more to ask

But except for one wish

“ Stay with me forever honey “♥?

Like the autumn wind blowing

Through the park

That the fallen leaves

Has been taken

I wish for you

To hug me so gently

But then suddenly

I heard my heart whispering

That you are holding me

In your arms already

On this beautiful morning

Dream of loving you

As perfectly for the first time

I want to love you deeply

For a long time

Love you until my heart stops beating

And let the angels hear

What my heart says

If living my life with you

Is a dream

How I wish

To never wake up

And be with you forever❤

I fly without wings

I have no wings, but I fly,

With lovely love I try,

To go inside of you like blood,

To make a love bed.

I am not for away, but within your thought,

To change you a lot,

To become your great man,

Like your deep fan.

My love is endless,

It is really selfless,

Begging your heart,

To live with you like my part.

I am a child,

When your smile is mild,

You are like a beautiful fish,

Giving me a long lasting kiss.

I can't forget you,

Your memory I chew,

To you, it's unknown,

When I cry alone,

Better than

What better than knowing you exist, nothing really is...

What better than that, all the facts point to nothing, What bliss!

Just to live to experience life, you know I'm right...

Remember when you were a kid, imagining your greatness...

You can be anything, that was your gift, even if you don't get it, you're still living...

Giving all the love in the world, girls are treated like a pearls, boys key to the world...

Than you get older, the planet seems colder..

But they tell you the truth, your parents taught you what to do...

You have clothes, and a roof over your head, and you get to sleep in a bed..

We feel that the best, this a testimony, but the only you need, keep going...

Money does buy everything, even love, but not the way you think..

A woman is taught to search for security, and you're lucky...

If she chooses you, men look for loyalty, and some are hoping..

To find, we all look for what we want, but goodness is not gone, stay strong...

We want a good life, but being alive is enough just to experience stuff...

What better than this, nothing is, we live to finish our traditions...

Waning Passion

Once burning lava cools into hardened stone,

Leaving me utterly perplexed, standing alone.

Our sun waxed hot, traveling across the sky,

Immersive blackness replaces it, but why?

We were bound together by love's golden chain,

Now broken links upon the sands of time remain.

Together we built a mountain fortress, safe and sound,

But it slowly implodes, leaving rubble on the ground.

Geezers of uncontrolled excitement irrupted faithfully,

Once impressive plumes barely bubble, disheartening me.

Unexpected changes in desire are quite extreme,

A torrential waterfall has become a trickling stream.

Passionate romance can we ever recapture, regain,

Or is it destined to slip away, continue to wane?

I seek explanations, council from mighty God above,

Is there any chance of saving a sadly fading love?

And she noticed she wants to be noticed,

But her pride only lets her go so far.

She just wanted to be wanted,

In this world where no one no longer cares to know who you really are.

She's a lonely star,...

But she shines brighter than ever before.

She's a lonely star,...

But she'll shine bright ever more.

Everything doesn't seem to be what she thought it was,...

She sees the world through brand new eyes.

And nothing will ever be the same,...

But she's got a brand new light, and it's blinding bright.

She's a lonely star,...

But she shines brighter than ever before.

She's a lonely star,...

But she'll shine bright evermore

We didn't meet by coincidence

You were the longing of my soul

You were the beat of my heart

You were the wish of my mind

You were the dream in my sleep

You were the desire of my senses

Our reunion was the beginning of a story

Crafted perfectly by destiny

Our hearts and souls merged

I became you, you became me

We became one

One of the greatest thing, I recently learned is to embrace, let go and even walk away from anything that upsets my peace of mind.

This short zen tale, explains it perfectly:

“If someone hands you over a gift and you don’t accept it, who owns the gift?» asks the Samurai.

“The one who tried to give it », answered one of his disciples.

“This also applies to envy, rage and hate, when they are not accepted, they always belong to the one who carries them in his heart», said the master

If I received a star each time

You touched my heart

You made me laugh

You showed me love

If I received a star each time

You tendered my soul

You filled my life

With colours and sunshine

If I received a star each time

You hugged me near

You swiped my tear

You erased my fear

If I gave you a star each time

I prayed the sky

To have you mine

We'd be holding now

All the stars of the night

A DREAM

A glimmer blinks from afar

It almost fades in the darkness

I move towards it

I hurry

I run

I'm still running...

The suffocation of the days increases

The whine of the years piles up

The memories of the past awake

The images of the ages pass by

And dreams travel...

I run

How your glimmer is away from my darkness

I run

Ages run

What a long nightmare

Where does it end

Where lies its truth?!

God! How beautiful is that glimmer

At the end of the world

At the end of the dream.

I feel it's her glimmer

Her hollow...

I see through it her purity, her chastity

The honesty of her love, the integrity of her vow!

It is her light

But is it the light of

Her longing soul

Or her fallen tears?!

I run

I thought I arrived

I'm surrounded by water

It almost covers me...

A running river.

I asked, they answered:

These are tears from her eyes...

Tired of separation,

They cried out of despair!

Forgive me, my goddess

I run, I row, I arrive

I see her

I scream, I approach, I hold her, I exalt

I lose consciousness!

It was a hollow

A fantasy...

An illusion...

It was nothing.

I open my eyes

I came back from the world of dreams

But there she is... beside me

A reality approaching me

I see her, I touch her, I hear her

It's her for real...

Am I in a dream?!

Wishful

I have those day, where I'm off on my way, in my brain

Wishing the same thing, someday someone will love me, funny

There are days I don't deserve it, but I'm not perfect..

I keep working on self, it help, well it's not enough, love

To be hugged, ugh, even talking would be a plus..

Must not give up, but fix up just for us whoever duh

After lust is over

Love is not an armour,

It grows well with rumour,

It dances in every tongue,

Like a peacock out of a ring.

No one knows how it comes and goes,

And how it blooms like a rose,

In the heart pool with imagination,

Without having communication.

Someone comes inside like a queen,

Giving joy, sorrow and pain,

Within the mind in the dreams,

Like the immortal love flames.

Is love pure or impure?

When the body becomes mature,

It is a trap of fantasy,

To escape from that it's not easy.

Everyone yearns for a lover,

Thinking that love is a beautiful flower,

One day it will fall down after lust is over,

Telling us that they have no lover.

We both don't know

How to tell what is right from wrong

We are both too lazy to ask

On how to separate

Between kindness and blame

When everything is like a floating cloud

Only love will last forever

In the oceans of love

Everything seems so right

We will never ask again

Whether it is worth loving or not

Nor even worrying about

Those things that losing of something

Because we both know

That we can find true love

Even in the sound of the wind

So why worry with the circumstances

If our heart will never change

Let's just think of our love

To be pure and last forever♥?

My Love,

My soul knows

That your love grows

In my heart it flows

Running through my veins

Watering me again and again

Sowing joy where there was pain

Our love story goes on

For it is written since the start

That our souls will never part

My heart keeps looking for you

My soul leads me your way

With you she wants to stay

With you she feels safe

Like a bird in its nest

Like the sun on the horizon rests

Listen to my pulse

It whispers your name

Listen to my soul

She echoes the same

You're my sunshine in the rain

To you my heart and soul pertain

My love,

My heart sings a love song

The music composed by my heartbeat

The words created by my mind

All orchestrated by my soul

Your love made me live in eternal spring

It filled my heart with butterflies

That fly over an endless field of red roses

My heart knows that you're the one

For only you stood by me in all stances

Swiping away my tears and sorrow

Pouring in tenderness and joy

Someday, I'll wear the white dress for you

Reflecting...

The peace of my heart

The light of my love

The purity of my intentions

The maturity of our relation

And the devotion of my soul

For you my sweet sweet love...

THE RETURN

I am exhausted by the long wait

Till I thought forgetfulness is the reality

And pain is my breath!

God! What do I see on the horizon

Something shining...

Is it a mirage that awakens hope in me?

Or a lost bird also looking for its lover?

I don't know why my heart dances with joy

Its pulse has changed its beat

Perhaps it's him... coming back...

After being devastated by separation!

Nothing separates us but eons and horizons

Waves and seas

Waiting and longings

And a hope after separation!

The wait is still long

It almost mocks me

And mocks my hope for his return

No... It's no longer a hope

It became a certainty

His vow to me was not dispelled by illusions

Nor tossed by the wind

Nor divided by ages

And it will not end at the edge of forgetfulness

For it is eternal.

So it was, and so it will remain!

That strange sparkle is approaching

My breath is accelerating with it

I can almost feel his own breath

Touching my face to warm the coldness out of loneliness!

Ages moved fast

Till a boat reaches the shore of love

From which he gets out...

My life companion!

I tried running towards him

But the load of hopes slowed my feet

Slowed my breath

Slowed time

So the eagerness to meet him felt

Almost suffocated...

I embraced him...

Why did you desert me?...

Why did you let the angel of death take me from you?...

Why did you let ages separate us?!

But...

My arms were embracing an illusion

A mirage that deceives my eyes

I fade in the illusion

In the nothingness

Within the atoms of voidness!

I woke up after a lifetime as known by our time

And see the dream fading away

The truth is becoming clear now

He is here, my life companion

By my side

Embodied in my reality

He is truth – the whole truth

POETRY

Poetry is not mere rhyme

Poetry is not mere words..

Poetry is the meaning of life

Poetry is the trump card..

Poetry adds value to heart

Poetry adds value to soul..

Poets takes us to the destiny

Poetry takes us to the goal..

Poetry heals all the sadness

Poetry heals all the plights..

Poetry gives the eternal freedom

Poetry gives the knowledge and light..

Poetry offers us the freedom and joy

Poetry offers us the happiness..

Poetry introduces us with the Mother Nature

And the blue sky which is endless..

Poetry teaches us the blessings of the mankind

Poetry teaches us the blessings of the humanity..

Poetry tells us to live together

With respect, love and unity..

What about us?

Lovers are getting married

What about us?

I dream of a little house

Lost in the woods

A place of inspiration

For writing and meditation

People are sharing vows

What about us?

Our hearts are in love

Our souls dream of

A permanent reunion

Crowned by their fusion

Our love is divine

Your heart is mine

Our souls are intertwined

What about us?

I am yours till the end of times

Love is love

Sweats on my skin,

When in my heart, you pin,

You face is a flower, you look is like a throne,

Prickling my heart, when you have gone.

I play with you when I doze,

My strength I often lose,

My tongue is not steady to chat,

When you appear in front of me like an art.

No word to speak,

My heart is so weak,

When your smile is like light,

Within me, it is so bright.

I know you were born for me,

You frequently come to see,

My presence from your home,

When in the street, I roam.

Women's hearts are deeper than oceans,

To men, they show different seasons,

Yet love is love, you can't forget,

Once in love you get wet.

And he told her ...

My love, promise me now

That you will forever remain

The lover of my life

My tender soulmate

The twin flame of my heart

I want you to read my eyes

Snatch me from pain

And hold me inside your heart

Let me stay near you

For I need to breathe through you

I miss you like a refugee misses his home

Promise me that you will never leave my hand

For how many times have I stubbed my pride

Going back to your heart

The same heart we both share

My life is enlightened by your proximity

You're my soulmate ... for eternity

My love,

Love was born for you and me

With you I learned love

With you my heart first felt love

For you my soul longs

To you my heart belongs

Only love will bring us closer

It tells me your heart's whispers

Our love is like a prayer

That has the power

To remove all barriers

Of fear, pain and despair

Our love is the light

That enlightens our path

With courage and faith

It sets our steps right

To keep holding on

Through tempest and storms

For true love never fails

It always prevails

A Cry for Help

The sea waves swash is almost deafening my ears

It's all I hear

Or is it perhaps the swash of hope in my heart?

I wish the waves of the sea would bring you back to me

So I would dry your body with the flames of my longing!

I wish death had forsaken me...

I wish I hadn't left you...

I wish I hadn't fallen asleep that night

And stayed awake by your side!

Forgive me my love

The mightiness of death was stronger than me

It stole me from my world

And from your world

It kept me away from your eyes

From my love...

Forgive me.

I hear your call coming from afar

An angelic whisper...

So I call you

The call dissipates through the sea waves

That take it far away

To all parts of the world...

But they don't return it

They fear to return empty-handed

To tell me that they didn't find you!

My love, when will you come back

So I may regain my life

And fill my existence with years of lost happiness

During which I lost myself too!

I dread sleeping

To avoid missing your come back and the passion of our reunion

I am awake since the night of our separation

Waiting...

I never got tired of waiting

You must come back

God has written in human's hearts:

There will be no separation between two lovers...

Even if separated by death

Or lost between realms!

I look at the horizon

And feel a numbness running through my limbs

Stealing my wakefulness and my day

Weakening my waiting

Suddenly I lost my life!

Darkness surrounds my soul

I feel more cold than the coldness of the graves!

Where are you my love?

Where is the warmth of your breath?

Had I known I will find you in this lonely dream

I would rather live in the coldness of graves

Than return to a life without your breath!

I inhale warmth into my being

A hope of reunion!

Please answer the call

Even by imagination!

She lived her whole life

With her own face

Didn't know life

Was a masquerade

She was heartfelt

With devotion she dealt

She gave love

And tenderness

Though within her

There was only

Voidness

Then one day her mind

Whispered to her:

Wake-up...

Can't you see

That you live in pain

For others don't feel the same

They see life as a game

They play with dice

But only you pay the price

For your heart is on the table

You are doing the impossible

For those not willing

To do for you even the possible

Wake up from your slumber

Keep your goodness

To those who deserve it

To those who reciprocate it

Who value your presence

In their life

Give yourself all that love

Withdraw from their game

Save your pride and dignity

Don't lose yourself

With absurdities

you left me there dear

you left me there

I stood and stood

hope to be rescued

like a child lost in the crowd

As blind be explained light

the crowd go on preach

it's simply a breach to fight

When silent nights fell into memories

The suffocating vacuum disappears

Tear that holds my ocean of pain

Never fills your hollow heart drops in vain

TAILING SPIRITS:

My love, where did you go?

Looking into the gloom in your eyes

I reach out to touch your cheek

But your reaction time is always first past the post—

Your hand already heft in the air,

And my face subject to scrutiny by your bulging eyes.

My hero is the benevolence that tugs at you,

Flooding your face with embarrassment

Drawing your daring hands back into the depths of your pocket.

I regain composure with your model monster gone,

Hiding beneath your skin.

I start counting days again,

Until you come home guttered, a bottle in one hand

And anger in the other, huffing and puffing your chest

As you wrestle me. . .

But even luck tires itself in time.

A monkey argues with a donkey

On the colour of grass

The monkey says it's green

The donkey insists it's blue

They resorted to the lion

Who acquitted the donkey

But punished the monkey

Banishing him from the forest

For a whole year

The lion said to the monkey:

Stubborn monkey

We all know that the colour

Of grass is green

Yet I am punishing you

Because you're arguing

With a donkey!

Moral:

Never argue with a fool!

Weep For Myself

I'll weep for myself I think

For you are not alone

Its me and mine here now

For you are not alone

I come and go

And cannot stay

It's hard to go

To stay away

From those I love

Day to day

From whom I need

From those I made

I never meant to hurt

I didn't mean to prey

I never ever thought

It would end in this way

To see you smile

And hear your joy

That in a while

You will enjoy

Another man

That is not me

Another man

To make you happy

It should be me

Or so I thought

It could be me

I could have fought

But it's gone I think

It is no more

And I feel that pinch

I know it's torn

You are my friend

But I'm not yours

You are my breath

I'm your lost cause

I'd bleed for you

Not let you fall

I'd die for you

And much much more

I do not matter

To you Sarah Jane

I wish I mattered

To you again

But you do not need

To hear all this

I should not plead

For what I miss

If I do not ask

If I don't try

You can't say yes

Only goodbye

Just A Burn In Me...

Come help me

Fight with me

Bring me...

Into your intellect

Your spoken dialect

So we can connect...

A time with you

Just being you

The very you...

Who brings your being

Into my seeing

Your literal feeling...

Of our time

That was a crime

Just a passing rhyme...

With a contrast

To be loved at last

From your past...

Unsinkable feelings

With no ceilings

You got me reeling...

It's in your finding

I find my whining

Is there love in dining?

Yeah...

Let's get a deal....

Deal on.....

Deal on ...

Deal on....

Feelings won't last long...

Deal on...

Deal on...

Deal on...

FAITH

Her hollow is everywhere

It prevails over the world

Moves in the realms of my existence!

I can only breathe through her breath

I only feel through her love

I am only exalted through her scent!

Forgive me, my goddess

Forgive my weakness

I wish my eyelids hadn't closed

I wish the sudden death hadn't taken me away from you!

Forgive me

I wish I could find you to kneel in front of you

To recite the prayer of forgiveness!

All over the earth I wander

Searching for my goddess

For the safe haven of my soul

I search for her everywhere

In all countries

In all times...

I glimpse her in the gracefulness of every butterfly

That caresses the sun rays with its wings...

I hear her voice in the chirping of every bird at dawn...

And I dream of her in the evening of every night...

My life has rather become a dream

In which I see her hollow

I approach towards her

I extend my arms to embrace her...

But

Can two hands hold a hollow?!

Can two fingertips capture a ray?!

When does the dream end?

I feel as if the last day is near

The blackness of the night is now even darker

I am short of breath

Shivering

Fear

Suffocation

Coldness

Frost

Loneliness...

And I surrender to the power of sleep

Or is it the angel of death?!

I succumb to a long slumber...

I search in the dream for her

I search in each corner of the dream for her hollow

For a clue that would lead me to her

For her scent that fills my life

For her smile that illuminates the darkness of my soul

To awake me from this frightening nightmare

And bring me back to her!

LONGING

Alone... feeling in exile from myself

I look around

I see nothing but barren spaces

I hear nothing but echo!...

The sea stretches to the horizon

My eyes are staring...

He may come on a ship

I will keep waiting for him

Even if I spend all my life just waiting!

My eyes are fixing the horizon

Forgoing anything else....

They await a hope,

A promise,

Freedom!

She's now captive

Captive of anguish and sorrow

Captive of time and place

Whenever a wave approaches the shore

She hears his call through its swash

Or the news of his coming

Whenever the wave returns to the sea

She hears his promise!

Where is my loving companion?

Why did he leave me in my carelessness and departed

Why did he create me out from his own existence

Then walked away from me?

Where is he?

I shiver from frost

Is it the moisture of sea water that has crept into my boredom?

Or is it the coldness of separation?

Why do I see nothing but a blue sea

With a boat on its waves

I fear it may sink!

My eyes aren't tired staring at the horizon

The horizon has become my haven...

My longing, my hope, my everything!

Where is he?

If only the waves of the sea would answer me

If only the heat of the sun would warm my heart

If only life would have mercy on me...

I hear his words in the whispers of the water's splash

In the opening and closing of seashells

In the soft laughers of seagulls

I hear his call from afar

Coming...

So I listen

I wait

The call still resonates

It's the echo

The echo of the past

The echo of the memory

The echo of forgetfulness

The echo of a love in pain!

INDISPENSABLE LOVE

Her love is beyond description,

Even to my own observation

I think she is the best satisfaction,

That deserve my attention

For her love intoxicate like wine,

With her I'll be fine

No doubt, she is mine,

For her love don't have a finish line

She fill my heart with happiness,

Her love still remain in excess

I'll never put her in darkness

Neither will I fill her heart with sadness

I'll never put her to shame,

Neither will I cheat or play game

Her love still remain the same,

That's the reason I still cherish her name

Her love is real and she is not fake,

For her love, I can jump into the lake

Even if she decide to betray,

My love for her will never decay..

"Bond of love"

...Shut not your bowel

Of compassion towards me...

...You're the sun destined

To wipe away the darkness

In me...

.. Grapple my love unto your soul

With hoops of steel...

...For our bond is more delicate

Than the air we breath...

WHAT I LOVE ABOUT YOU

I love your charming smile,

The way it comes with style,

I can run a thousand mile,

Just to see you with my eyes,

I love your figure 8,

I swear you drive me crazy,

But now it's too late,

You're now my fate,

I love your beautiful soul,

Filled with life and love,

I'm only whole,

When you fill my heart's empty hole,

I love your gladdening voice,

Each time I hear it,

It mesmerizes with my thoughts,

And I can't help but to rejoice,

I love the times we spend together,

Under the cold and hot weathers,

Provided you're with me,

I do not care nor bother,

I love you and everything about you,

I hope in due time,

Everything comes through,

And my dream of you comes true.

A blessed man,

With a blessed pen??,

LOVE'S GONE.

All these years,

I stayed beautiful

On the inside and out

For you...

While you looked somewhere else,

I gave you my

Humble and loving heart,

Couldn't you have been nice a bit

You crushed it

While giving yours to someone new

My shoulder was always

There for you to cry on

But my back;

You rode like a horse to dirt

Like a jar of milk, am split

You wanna know why it

Turned out this way?

I did all I could not to let

This animal in me out,

I can't hold it back no more...

For my love; you toyed with,

For the strength; you took off me

For that beauty in me you never saw,

You sure going to get a feel of this ugly animal you've let out.

I Wish This Love Will Last

In the dew of this morning,

To help you is my duty,

If wish can come true,

I wish we live forever,

I rather die than be apart,

What an adorable love?

Love full of compassion,

Exotic feelings oozing,

The lady I adore is in me,

In the castle of my heart,

Loving you is most,

For my life is attached to you,

I wish this love will last,

I pray it last to eternity,

If love is crime,

I am the most wanted criminal,

If love is a thief,

You have stolen my heart,

Your love is magnificent,

A jewel and a gem,

I can't afford your price,

But you dashed me your heart,

I am thankful,

For you and love,

WALLS OF LOVE

"The rhythm of your heartbeat

is the only music that appeals

my soul." She said,

" I replied",

The only thing I want in life is

to be known loving you.

We hugged, kissed and said in

unison, "let our names be written

on the walls of love."

UNDESCRIBABLE.

How will I describe my life ever since I met you,

I don't even know what love means until you came out of the blue,

You and me become super tight like paper and glue.

You gave me hope that love truly existed,

Even when I am completely dried your love keep me hydrated,

When you are afar, I feel your love so close,

I feel pain when I miss you cause you have been like a daily dose.

For love you are the only one that understand me through,

Even though in my heart several thought brew,

Your sparkling eyes and smiles took me so far.

You amplify my joy and drain,

Out my pain,

It took me sometime for me to realize,

Real love is not something you advertise.

I love you more each day,

Without you it is impossible to stay,

When I has what it meant to feel this,

I was told I had trip for love,

I have been tied up with love,

Cause it has made me as pure as dove.

My love for you is undescribable,

The joy you brought is undetectable.

Fall in love_

I fell in love with a thief, he stole my heart away.

I fell in love with a jailer, he caged my heart in his.

I fell in love with a cop, he shot me, I didn't die but I smiled.

I fell in love with a photographer. Such a sharp shooter. He blinked. My heart melt. Eyes met. I fell.

I fell in love with a singer, my life; such an exquisite song with romantic lyrics.

I fell in love with a cobbler, he shines my heart, it glitters.

I fell in love with a plumber, everyday my heart pumps, he repairs every hole in my heart. I'm so glad.

I fell in love with a navy, my soul turns blue, I was glued. My heart joyfully boom.

I fell in love with a painter, he paints my name on the sky with colours of the rainbow.

I fell in love with a poet, I became his muse, in every lines and stanzas, I portray the beauty of Melissa.

I fell in love with nature, the flowers I nurture, it beautifully blooms. I sail through the ocean. I bath in the waterfall. The mountain; my abode.

I fell in love with the sky, I built my mansion on the cloud, the moon became my couch, I wore the stars around my neck.

I fell in love with me; a beautiful being, a beauty decked with purity. With a pure heart, tender like snowflake. A pure smile. Crystal clear. Stare. I'm love.

A Night with You

Let me sneak some moments of love with you.

Let me steal you from you.

Barricading all your worries behind

And taking you to a world of mine.

And keep you with me for the time being.

Come, sit under this star-studded sky.

Let these stars and night on our eternal love pry.

Can I lie in your lap here?

Let us feel each other

Leaving no gap there.

I want to drown in you wholly.

Wanna refill your ears with our endless stories jolly.

And tickle your memory with our love sweet-bitter.

I want to let you hold my hand .

And make new promises of future

Keeping past ones in blend.

Let me cause you thunder of laughter.

Keeping my silly jokes in your empty plate.

Let me lie in your arms for the whole night.

And let our love get recharged and further ready to thrive.

Let this night never cease to exist.

So shall our eternal love be!

A Poem: Love

Sometimes I wonder how we got entangled

I want to hate and love you

My crush with a velvety voice

You give oxygen to my soul

And bring me beautiful "somethings"

Beyond the lucid cloud

I see a picture in a glass

Carefully tucked therein is your statuesque frame

With glossy ruby red lips.

If I wander away like the lost sheep

Please call me back

For I may have lost my mind.

Forget the merchant men from the rear

They are destroyers of temples;

They claim to be merchants from Venice.

What they seek is whom to devour

While they move to the next game.

I am the real deal Sugar Love!

Like you see with the Crocs. And Hippos

I am not gunning for the waters of frivolities.

What I want is your heart my Heart.

I want to be your morning star and shining light.

Somehow, you know you want me too

Please quit the "Stop it, I like it"

Even if you have a mouth that cuts like a blade

Flaws that make you distinct and natural

Even if you are the offspring of Dangote

A nephew to Bill Gates my heart will still yearn for you.

In this game of love we shall win if we believe!

Love hurts

Love has hurt us all

Making us walk in our naked shames

For those who know our names

Have used love to kill our fame

Leaving us with with dark fate

As no where to hide our naked shameful face

Love is all lies

But it depends what lies in the hearts

As am from a town that love lies

Which kills the innocent flies

I hate love

I hate it more

Cause I cry all night long

Love love has treated me wrong

Love has sang a sad song

With the drums of sorrow songs

Sing those song of forever together

As in any kind of weather

My love will not bitter

But stand in all storms of every weather

Your love is fake

Your kiss fade

I wish I never give you

My virgin heart for you to use and dump

I wished I never loved you

KAYODE

Dear Kayode my lover,

How do I metaphorize your love?

Holding you and leaning on you,

Kissing and looking into your eyes,

Without caring that Mama was watching,

Standing at the door with her long stick.

Dear Kayode my lover,

Should I still trust your love from the bush,

Where you made me feel like a woman,

Not minding that I gave you what's considered precious,

Pricking ourselves with a needle to prove our love,

Even when Mama had warned me severally about you.

Dear Kayode my lover,

You didn't take me with you when leaving for Lagos,

You didn't come, even after we planned to meet under that tree,

I still go there, hoping to see you there one day,

And stay there from dawn till dusk,

Even when Mama comes to flog me to go to the farm,

I waited like a stubborn fly, waiting to follow the corpse to the grave.

Dear Kayode my lover,

I was sick and mama said I'm pregnant,

I haven't seen my August visitor in a while,

So I guess she's right, we're having our first baby,

But you're not here to give me support,

Mama threw me out of the house and called me a slut.

Dear Kayode my lover,

I saw you when the midwife said push,

I leaned on your unforeseen strength as I birthed our child,

I named him Kayode because he looks exactly like you,

I never forget to tell him about you, and our love,

Dotting the I's and crossing the T's till he crossed twenty-one.

Dear Kayode my lover,

I am dancing bata as our son is getting married,

I never forgot to go to our sacred tree,

Where I wish to die and be buried, as my final wish,

Kayo's children are playing in the compound,

Yet I never lost hope of seeing you again.

Dear Kayode my lover,

I am now six feet into the ground,

My corpse now decomposed by the worms,

If ever you look for me,

I am at that tree, sleeping while waiting for you,

Don't forget to bring my favourite flowers, I'll be waiting.

You keep telling me you'd never love me .

I'd never be enough for you .

We can never be together .

You'll never be mine.

In your hatred I found love ,

In your hatred I found the truth.

Don't tell me to quit trying .

Cause you know I would never .

I might not deserve you ,

But all I ask for is your love .

In my love you'll find peace ,

If only you give it a trial.

If it takes you years to say those three words.

I'll be eager to hear them .

But don't take too long dearie .

I might not be able to wait forever.

Life without love is like

Home without mother

Life without love is like

Lock without key

Life without love is like

Bird without feathers

Life without love is like

Dinner without dessert

Life without love is like

Smile without shine

Life without love is like

Cricket without umpire

Life without love is like

Competition without judge

Life without love is like

Movie without climax...

Unseen

Secret sorrows

Which the world

Knows not

I don't fancy

Furthermore

Try, try, try again stuff

I've owned it

I just want out

I am so drained

So twenty

And so far

So am I

exhausted

for the millionth time

in my being I wish

smallpox or some other

effortlessly

understood disease

rather the

internal bleeding

be acknowledged

is so heavy

all the time

that I can't get away from it

not ever

the whole story is: I am empty

my cerebrum

Don't fall in love too fast.

Because the truth is, when you fall in love fast,

It's not love.

Nothing good in our lives comes fast.

When you fall in love too fast you think, you

Know them very well, you think know their

Dreams but you only know their mind.

Don't just give away your trust, let someone earn

It. Because remember, you can't eat the fruit of

The seed just because you planted the tree.

Ps: what's love got to do, got to do with it?

AFTER A DECADE

The meet was unexpected as they met after ages,

Tears ran down from her beautiful sparking eyes

Her lips were trembling and his heart was

Pounding.

His thumb moved gently across her wet cheeks

Before both his hands moved up to cradle each

Side of her face as he slowly lowered his head

And claim the softness of her lips with his own.

A kiss so poignantly beautiful impossible not to

Respond as his lips gently sipped and tasted his

Own.

His hands leaving the sides of her face as he

Drew up into his arms,

Both realised they'd worn in each other nerves

And emotions and heart in all these passing years

They are made for each other no matter how

Different are their ways.

The feelings that had been buried for years

The words which are left unsaid before a decade

Unfolded when their soul mate and lust and love

Collide.

It took away all the pain and worries

And waiting for each other was worth it.

Every single word said by you were cogent,

You were not just smart, but intelligent,

Always excited to meet you at the station,

There were few words that gave a name to our

Relation.

I always enjoyed chatting with you,

I always liked talking about you,

I always loved speaking for you,

The only words left unsaid was "I Love You".

Without further delay let's express our feelings,

I have a lot to speak without any ceilings,

Gave up my everything for the person I cared,

Many memories left unuttered I wished I could

have shared.

Lost nights when we had fights,

Just had a crash with the memories like trash.

Just want you to confess that you are all alone,

I will come rushing towards your side; when you will feel like.

If you were ever mine, this decision won't take time..

I'll be waiting till the end till you know about this hell,

I hope a day comes when you'll say, "Yes! You're mine, you are the human version of my sunshine".

Even at my mess, I'll love you the best!

It seems to be a heart shattering yesterday,

But it's been a long run without a shadow,

It's like someone divided the heart into pieces and none of us is at peace!!

Some relationships are as fragile as glass, If they

are not taken care of, you get broken, If jealousy

lies in relationships then, they don't get formed

and get shattered. then try to cover the many

Times but these are not the same as before.

If you are in love, then express it .

not one time try to hundred times, you must

have done it successful .

if you prepare yourself. for some relationships.

confessions your mistakes ,you will wander a

little, but spend your life.

Loving is poison

I keep falling in again, falling in again, its dragging me down, i know, by joining, that its only gunna end, only gunna end with me on the ground, im begging dont go, im begging dont go, dont go for the good of us, im begging dont go, im begging dont go, dont go for the good of us,

Used to beg me to stay but now you're leaving, maybe this your way of getting even, cause I've been sitting on these flights, all the messages I write, sometimes wonder if you took the time to read em, like is this really what its come too, especially after everything we stuck through, an maybe you're right you ever loved me, but you're losing somebody who truly loves you, I cant lie that hurts, a feeling that is only ever gonna get worse, I can barely find words, I just need you right here, how's it take only a second to erase a whole year, this was always my fear, an I guess it was right, now all I do is think about you every night, an I cant take no more,

Loving is poison, i keep falling in again, falling in again, its dragging me down, i know, by joining, that its only gunna end, only gunna end with me on the ground, im begging dont go, im begging dont go, dont go for the good of us, im begging dont go, im begging dont go, dont go for the good of us

I told you what hurts me the most and you did it perfectly, I told you what hurts me the most, and you did it,

Loving is poison, i keep falling in again, falling in again, its dragging me down, i know, by joining, that its only gunna end, only gunna end with me on the ground, im begging dont go, im begging dont go, dont go for the good of us, im begging dont go, im begging dont go, dont go for the good of us.

Hi. Sorry I haven't texted you back. I've been anxious and depressed. I haven't had time to catch my breath,you know how life gets. I am so drained I cannot can't even collect energy for the most basic tasks. Like texting you back or washing tan dishes. The weather has been beautiful right? Yesterday I fought off a panic attack while driving and had to pull over because my vision was blurred. I just want to sleep all the time, but if I told you, you would just want to uncover a reason behind all this, and there is no tangible reason you would accept as valid. How are you? I hope well.

Let's get dinner soon...

It's not for the first time That I don't know where do words rhyme But it's not the same, I can bet from the vibe That feeling of loneliness And all the life that's been a mess Seems like a game of chess A wrong move and everything is gone

Mistook early sunset as dawn And when the wind told me stories Of all the things those were just worries

I think I cannot hold it anymore For the storm was just near the shore Everyone ran as they saw it gear But I stood there without any dear Could not guess what happened then For I was surrounded by no men

"His grip on her was firm, solidly guiding. She could feel the strength of his hands against her flesh, not really rough, but not exactly gentle either. He positioned her where he wanted her and made it clear that she should stay still. His hand on her shoulder. His grip on her hip. When he entered her, the way he filled her and stretched her made her feel breathless.

He controlled her body. He focused her mind."

- **Purely Erotic Visions**

Unsaid Confessions :

Feeling are enriching multiple vibes,

Heart goes crazy for her looks,

Mind finds different ideas and confusions,

Words struck in me for her beauty,

Still my love for her is unsaid confessions.

Trying for best to convey her,

But I hesitate a lot to express,

Mind says I can express her,

But heart says you can't,

Feelings in deep goes around,

Deep inside myself in love,

Hiding Myself for unknown reasons,

Hoping for best to get great time,

To confess my feelings without hesitation.

Modern Love Story

What we can call,

To this love story?

Both are online for each other,

But no one texting first sorry.

What we can call,

To this love story?

Both side love is true so,

But both person having much ego.

What we can call,

To this love story?

From both no one said sorry,

They started continuing their regular hobby.

What we can call,

To this love story?

Both can't live without fondness of each other,

Because they are actually true lovers.

They haven't met face to face in life,

Just on Phone They made millions of vibes,

As they became love birds on social platform,

Their distance from each other is far long.

So what we can call,

To this love story?

Nothing much but,

"A Modern Love Story."

"Love when suppressed gives a reminder always and would be etched in brain as memories. Love feels good both for the one who bestows it and the one who receives it. Even the subdued self yearns to work for the other .Love erupts as lava when the occasion occurs, no matter the situation."

One mortal expression of my immortal love.

Keeping aside the repository of repercussions.

Thick maybe a canopy but beneath lies the

beauty.

Your one photo shakes my equilibrium,

a tranquillizer of my world still without you.

Soothing is that prick for I know,

one day you will come through.

Your eyes are so stealthy and when ours met,

mine shushed my heart.

Slaying is your look, scrambled by grey emotion,

Dear I'd still love black and white.

All that my mind makes is a pizzicato to all that

our hearts have grazed.

Every pluck, stings the pangs of shrewd me,

notes of that pluck discard harmony as of now.

You the bridge, I the string, our love the bow.

I feel the pizzicato should turn into a cordless

rhythm.

Actually it creates wonders for me.

You are the purest,

You are the simplest,

You rule over me.

Dear Heart.

Never be depressed as there would be some king

who will you.

And there are my parents living within you,

So please take care of yourself.

Oh Dear Darling,

I Love You.

This pain of not letting out pain

I don't know why I refrain

From doing what I intend to

Suddenly everything seems blue

The words get caught

And they really push a lot

The fear of losing my dear ones

Is the cause of losing myself

Twilight embraced the night while darkness engulfed the vicinity. She welcomed it like an old comrade, who cried with her, tears of despair or rather like an enemy against whom she fought an unseen battle.

Tucked away in her bed, she looked at the clock longing for promising dawn or was it a desire for the caressing hands of death, which could end this intimate suffering. Slowly, hollowness began to fill her being, a tightening knot formed in her gut while her heart sank into unknown depths.

A wave of numbing pain took over as muted cries permeated the shadowed room. Her whole being quivered, as she battled with the silent screams from within. Sunlight peeped through the window and kissed her good night.

Choking on tears,
Nostalgia hitting hard,
Torn between knowing facts and accepting them,
Trying to avoid the clichés,
But life isn't getting any easier,
But how do I avoid what's pulling me low?
How do I accept my life that lies ahead of me
without the ones I have dreamt eternity with?
Some bonds are made by choice,
But some bonds were made even before I knew I
had a choice,
How do I subside the outrage erupting within
me?
How to count on my courage when you were my
pillar of strength?
How to pass this darkness when you've always
been my light?

How to overcome my grief when you were my

streak of happiness?

How to lift myself when you've been my

support?

How to convince my mind like you always won

my heart?

How to resist thinking about you when your

presence is missed?

How to let you know I loved you more but that

more was just not enough for you to stay?

Will I ever stop thinking about you?

Will my mind ever co-operate?

Will I ever stop feeling for you?

Will my heart ever listen to me?

Before I knew the world, the friends, the

happiness, the miseries, the rollercoaster rides, I

did pass coz I had you.

But today when I know the world, the friends,
the world of emotions stranded before me,
I look back for you, only to find that eternity is
incomplete without you here with me.
How does it feel to be spiralling amidst the
unpredictable storms with the waves of agony
surfacing and the winds of nostalgia taking a toll
against my heart?
No matter how much I let myself know I can't
have you like I did, well who doesn't like to be
the pampered sibling, do I have a chance to erase
the memories if I can't have you back?
I have only memories, and that's the hassle
I cannot run away from them,
It may sound selfish but only I know how much I
miss you ,
I wish I could rewind time and let myself know

that this wasn't for real and I have woken up

from a nightmare while weaving some beautiful

dreams.

I can only wish, I can only dream of having a

conversation like this with you,

"You came back? "

"I promised didn't I ?!

"Things could have been different you know.

You didn't have to fall so far! "

"I didn't. I didn't mean to.

This wasn't what I wanted. "

I can only wish to have you to stay with me and

that's what keeps hurting me.

I don't know when I have lost that happy go

lucky girl I used to be?

Then I remember I had you every time to wipe

my tears away, to share my victories with you,

watch you be proud of me every time. But what about today?

Unknown feelings of love

If a writer falls in love,

then she wrote about her cove.

His positive vibes will force her to write,

Dear ! Hold your pen tight , it's still night

Love finds its way,

Doesn't need to say.

Two unknown persons Meet ,

doesn't stay.

But love finds its way,

After go away.

Without love,

Roses don't have value.

Without love ,

Love stories don't exist.

Without love ,

Care can't be raised.

Infact without love,

life doesn't happy.

"You are important to me

As melody is important for a composition"

"you are in me

As lyrics are to a song"

"I feel you

Just like a musician feels the rhythm"

"I cant be completed without you"

"just like the composition cant be completed

Without a beautiful melody"

"May be I never see again

All the moments are flowing like rain" "your eyes

touch me

That's all I gain"

“yes I still love you rather than pain” “I always want you to be free Rather than putting you in chain” “I travelled all the way

Just to see you

Just by train”

“but still wish

I can see you again”

"Hhuh..!! I am just pissed of you, Leave me alone" I said him in anger.

We thought we will get back to each other but the misunderstandings between us was not going to make things works between us. We were best friends but I started loving him like lovers. Whenever & wherever he was with another girl I got hurt. I can’t even explain my feelings to him because I thought I will lost my best friend but I chose to stay with him and we were back with same bond. I don't know whether its love or something else but he was the one with whom I can't fake my emotions. The way he make efforts just to make me smile, the way he easily understood my unsaid words I wish I could confess him but I was scared so, it left unsaid and never explained & feelings can be left unexpressed. Unsaid words can mean anything and everything

Your story

Every single detail of yours

I would remember

Each conversation of ours

I would think back to

I would ask myself what this could be

what we could be

But then I know you're forbidden

Your someone I can't see

I hated the daylight

cause I had to keep away

You would look at me

but only at night

I was vulnerable and

you only cared about yourself

I wanted you for you

but you wanted me for you

Everything you said

that you wanted was against us

You saw us versus you

While I saw you and only you

You would act like we don't exist

Only to crawl back when the darkness persists

I believed you when you told me

You were hiding us and not me

That this bond was too special for the world to

see

I lost myself loving you

But with each circumstance that came by

you picked yourself

You made me believe in forever's

and now I don't believe in being together

I could never look through

what I made of myself

even after losing you

The damage remained with me

I kept revisiting and reminiscing my past with

you

How I wish I knew

that you were far from my moon

You were just a dark cloud

that led on a storm

in which I lost myself

A rain of unhappiness poured over me

and tears that added to your victory over me

and my defeat over myself.

Oho my love !When you were far and distant

away from me

My heart could feel Ur presence

Now, your close enough to me ,

Still my heart wanders to feel your presence

around me .

Your love and care towards me ,should

always bring wings to my happiness

But it shouldn't be a cage

that prisons all the happiness of my life .

WHO KNOWS

Who knows, I cry at night

Who knows, I fight for my right

Who knows, I kills my happiness for heavy price

Who knows, I might be sleep

Who knows, I don't like this or that

Who knows, I just want peace

Who knows, I hardly fulfil my wish

Who knows, I don't like lies

Who knows, I don't want to live

Who knows, I want to die

In a searching of my own Desires

Outside, the persistent calls of a wavering summer ,

Drudgery takes it claim, I find, I'm flightless, time catches me in a hypnotic dance. September melts into October, and paper stays paper, although my thoughts had blotted it's skin, once.

Months fly by like carriages and trains, whistles echoing,

a hundred million windows for watching space
but no time to measure moments, words, and all
the books I'm supposed to read before I turn
sixteen.
Days mould into nights and all that is left is a
heavy heart and a big eyed owl contemplating
stars wondering and dreaming
Clocks race until sleep is a welcome friend,
night time chews my mind into pieces. Outside,
time stretches like the sea, cold and unfeeling.
Tomorrow perhaps the sun will stay up longer ,
if I tell the clouds what I'm dreaming .
Through the misty eyes of the telescope I saw
love, and never realized it ,
Amidst the dark void of the sky ,
I saw hope and never pursued it..
Chased love in the form of lads and lasses,

chased hope in the form of wealth and fortune.

Yet, was blind to what was in front of me and

then alas, destiny stopped her pining.

For my hope was Earth's lover, the moon. And

my love ? It was for the dazzling array of

ethereal bodies,

The Planets ....

I had a chance to say!

I should have said it during our first meet!

Alas! I should have said it before the last fight!

Without a word uttered,

He left the world and me!

This word has many unsaid things,

His Love, Her pain

His agony, Her Fear,

His Pleasure, Her missing,

His Tears and ....

Her Death!

Yeah, I'll be honest

It's been like three months of no talking Walking by myself, no more eyes to get lost in Keep on looking back all the time

I hate being alone At least I got my conscience

Since you left me here

Locked up in my room Writing all these songs Wake up every morning And turn my computer on Because how else do I deal With these thoughts of you and me I was on the clouds Now I'm spiraling into the sea

I wrote a message for you But I couldn't send it

I regret it, yeah

I'm sorry I'm pathetic What's this? Caught a sickness And won't be getting better The sun might be shining But it feels like rainy weather, yeah

I try to keep it on the low I try to get you off my mind I try to keep my feelings inside (inside) But it's hard sometimes

loved - powfu I could neveryea

I thought with you it might work out But I guess I was wrong again I'm not sure what it is with me I've never been good with friends...

“”What’s meant to be will be.’

“No,’ I replied.

‘It’s what keeps you up at night, unable to sleep, and your chest tight, unable to breathe, your thoughts mad with desire and longing and your each and every waking moment pursuing what you desire with purpose and fury and aspiration-you cannot wait on destiny’ I said,

‘It’s presence must be demanded.””

Love is a weakness

Love smells like chlorine, Though, we want to dive in .

The real meaning of gentleman is not wearing proper dress . The man who always being kind and gentle with his surrounded people let me tell a story to you ..

I have two friends one male one female and what’s the special in this is both of them are in love for past 3 years and all the things where going properly in that time one day they fight with each other very time the problem is from boy but this time mistake is from girl.

The mistake is that she has talking to someone without informing to his boyfriend .. you are thinking that is not a problem. yes, there is no problem or mistake in that but there is a mistake in boyfriend's mind.

He had a doubt on his girlfriend that she cheating him but she not doing that and suddenly he blocked her number .

She had no clue on it and she said her friends to tell him unblock her but this not worked and he blocked everyone final she made a decision. She type a random number and tell her problem and ask to help her. One as accept it but one person try to convince the boy and tell about her and problem and explain to him and begged him to unblock her and he did not that she gone to depression.

After many days the boy meet a person that the person who talk with girl and know the truth and tried to call her but the call not reaching because gone to unknown world that we can't reach.

In this story the gentleness is not in dress in your behaviour and in your mind-set...

A Shelter for Life...

A shelter for life was all I thrived,

Even in the darkness I cried.

Even when the apocalypse arrived,

A shelter was what I couldn't derive.

First came the white horse, called himself Conquest;

To spread diseases and end its quest. Then came the red horse, called himself War, whatever was left to survive was brought to dust and the apocalypse wasn't far.

As they ripped Mother Earth and wanted more
to feed their pride.
Thus, came Famine, the black horse with paucity
while I cried. Still, I searched for a shelter to live.
And they said, “My child, we have nothing to
give.”
As humanity disappeared, I could only wait for
the last horseman to appear.
And I thrived for shelter with sweat and blood,
quietly in despair.
Mother earth was shattered, and the horsemen
turned out to be an absolute belter.
The shelter was nowhere to be found
and life was leaving this body without any sound.
Then, came Death and twitched in my ears,
“Live”, he said, “I am coming.”
That’s all I was desperate to hear and get rid of

the pain I couldn't bear.

At last Death finally arrived and I sighed, "Father!

I have been waiting so long for you here. "

I don't wanna say too much 'cause I'm weird I don't wanna tell you things that you'll fear I can say I'll wait for you but won't stay I can make promises but they'll break

I can say I care for you but won't cry I can pick flowers out but they'll die I can say I'll do my best and not change I can make promises but they'll break (ay, yeah, ay)

Gone with the wind I got something I cannot say now Flying to abyss I'm feeling nauseous on the way out You can put me down but I'm a different (personality) Spend a lot of time online cause I don't like reality

Yeah now I'm dazed and confused Why you here? You should leave my room You're so beautiful and perfect I don't understand my purpose

I don't wanna say too much 'cause I'm weird (I don't wanna say too much) I don't wanna tell you things that you'll fear (tell you things that you'll fear) I can say I'll wait for you but won't stay (no I won't stay) I can make promises but they'll break (promises but they'll break)

I can say I care for you but won't cry (I don't care at all) I can pick flowers out but they'll die (please don't let these

Die) I can say I'll do my best and not change (promises will break)

I can make promises but they'll break (I'm in love with you)

I need you more than ever...

THROUGH MY WINDOW – (INSPIRED)

Romantic drama takes a fair shot at a complicated teenage love story. What makes Through My Window watchable is its true-to-life narrative. It portrays the awkward, sexually charged romance between Raquel and Ares in all its human failing glory, and does so in a believable manner.

The messy feelings of the young teenage heart aren't easy to explain, let alone capture. The strength of this Spanish film lies in the fact that one can identify with it. Even though they are neighbours, Raquel and Ares belong to two vastly different worlds. The former is a regular middle-class high school kid who has aspirations to be a writer like her late father. The latter comes from the privileged Hidalgo business family. Raquel has harboured a crush on Ares for quite a while, going to the extent of gathering any information she can find on him. Ares is very aware of this infatuation and hacks into her Wi-Fi network as a ruse to strike up a conversation. The hacking of this Wi-Fi password is at the center of the attraction storm that is to follow between the two.

In spite of the characters' relatively young ages, the writer succeeds in detailing an underlying complexity to both their personas. Galle's standout performance infuses in Raquel a questioning ability beyond her years. Her writerly mind tells her not to get involved with her neighbour, and that he is bad news, but her attraction cannot be kept in check. The young actress portrays this complicated place one often finds themselves in exceptionally well. Though Peña isn't as effective, Ares' reluctance to admit his true feelings (beyond the physical) is presented adequately.

Through My Window, at its core, is based on a simple premise. Two teens fall hard for one another. It starts off bordering on the obsessive and gets real very quickly after that. While one of them isn't afraid to confront the full extent of her feelings, the other gets cold and distant after physical intimacy (making it look like the whole business is nothing but a fling). Ares tries hard to convince himself that Raquel is just another one of his long line of conquests. When that fails, he tries buying into his family's idea of things; he is being groomed to take over the business with his brothers after studying at Stanford, there's no time to get involved in the messy business of love, and so on. His cold father doesn't mince his words when he says to Ares, "Sleep with as many women as you like, but don't get involved with her."

Ares is torn between his reputation of being a carefree teen playboy and his undeniable affection for the girl next door. Whereas Raquel documents her on/off situation with Ares into a journal, creating an engaging narrative. And yet, at writing class, she never once volunteers to read out from her work. The fear and conflict experienced internally forms the crux of the story. Through My Window is charged with much sexual tension, and the filmmakers do not shy away from presenting its leads engaging in graphic physical scenes.

Unlike many other teenage romantic dramas, it doesn't build into this crescendo of blissful fantasy, as the concerned characters share their first unforgettable kiss as the end nears (or something along those lines). In that regard, the film is raw and real. Just because the lead characters have had sex multiple times, doesn't by any means suggest that there's a happily-ever-after on the horizon. The complexity of emotions on display mirrors that of an adult crowd and their complicated brush with the L word.

Maybe the makers could have toned down the explicit scenes a tad bit, but that's only a minor criticism. The film may not be in the same league as a Call Me By Your Name, for instance, but it certainly places high up on the scale of teenage love stories. The writing and acting are on point, providing the narrative with maturity, which is way beyond the years of its young cast. That it doesn't go down the oft-beaten path is also one of its hallmarks. Even though it isn't masterpiece material, it is a good film that has the ability to make you buy into love as a concept while not shying away from all the complexity that emotion.

Four Four Four:

Toa, Taoism, Tantra

Esoteric, I am sharing with you

Sexual energy abundantly clear

Touched erotically, sensually

No conflict of interest here

Enrapturing mind, body and soul

Releasing all sensibilities

Our chakras aline

Seven plus seven, Fourteen

A universal conjunction

Bodily on fire, wet and wild

Feelings unimagined

Psychotomimesis ensues

Your addicted, but free

Naked in every degree

Held gloriously in an orgasmic limbo

There on the edge

Breath taken, blood pumping

Ready to explode

An existence beyond erotica

Sexuality cultivated

Passions pursued and perpetuated

Lost to space and time

A celestial alphabet, profound

Not stopping at G

Pleasures traveling through every fibre

Like a freight train in slow motion

Off the rails, but in real time

All unconscious, coveted, desires

Consciously brought into place

A rhythm divine, we cum

Sacred geometry transpires

Four, four, four

Come, quench the once unquenchable.

Unravel the verses that linger

Yet remain misconceived, thaw the frozen!

Smouldered and left to rot in the open,

The pages within wither.

Alas, white lends to yellow.

Descry the thoughts,

Once labelled a masterpiece of rancid air!

A lover's delight yet a puritan's despair!

Delve further than the rest and unearth

Betwixt the facade of dolour,

A victim of a misshapen script.

Wherein my dearest,

The lead truly lies un-compared.

The smell of yours, from your shirts I wear;

The essence of your presence in my room;

The warmth through your body seeping into me;

The whispers of your touch on my skin,

Reminds you, though you are not here;

Holding your heart with mine,

Breathing for our love,

Clutching my chest to keep you there,

I still hope that you shouldn't leave me alone;

But, with your memories pumping in my heart,

With your love flowing in my veins,

I love you a lot that it hurts to let you go;

I love you a lot that it keeps me alive;

I love you, my love.

And I miss you.

For a human being, one of the essential nature is to talk. However, at certain times, a person may not able to talk due to certain reasons. Since we all know that we all have a shorter life, so we should not waste any time to say the important things. And if we are not able to do that, the words left unsaid will sit inside our mind screaming, i.e. it can be painful at some instances.

But sometimes words left unsaid is better than to say such words that can hurt other's feelings.

So people should be careful while speaking anything to others.

However, if a person understands you, then he/she will understand the words left unsaid.

Don't you know the knock of snow ,
Heavy legs and how it flows ,
Bloody Bloomberg Bloomington brow ,
And how it scares my flamingo ,
How I row to pass my row ,
How unlikely is the black crow ,
Xoxo my Xavier pinto ,

So remember whenever you feel low ,

I am there for you hitting the toe ,

But be careful while catching the dove ,

Because it is a symbol and matter of love. @improvkaar

INSPIRED BY

An acclaimed writer, his ex-wife, and their teenaged children come to terms with the complexities of love in all its forms over the course of one tumultuous year.

Meet the Borgens. William Borgens is an acclaimed author who hasn't written a word since his ex-wife Erica left him 3 years ago for another man. In between spying on Erica and casual romps with his married neighbour Tricia, Bill is dealing with the complexities of raising his teenage children Samantha and Rusty. Samantha is publishing her first novel and is determined to avoid love at all costs – after all she's seen what it has done to her parents. In between hook ups, she meets "nice guy" Lou who will stop at nothing to win her over. Rusty, is an aspiring fantasy writer and Stephen King aficionado, who is on a quest to gain 'life experiences'. He falls for the beautiful, but troubled Kate and gets his first taste of love and a broken heart. A tale of family, love (lost and found), and how endings can make new beginnings. There are no rewrites in life, only second chances.

—Becker Film Group

Published novelist Bill Borgens has a modicum of fame, especially within literary circles. He has fostered in his two offspring, nineteen year old college student Samantha Borgens, and sixteen year old high schooler Rusty Borgens, a love of writing in he making them keep journals since they were young to express whatever was on their mind, he never reading them unless asked. Bill himself has stopped writing in obsessing over his ex-wife, the children's mother, Erica, who left him for a younger man, Martin. While he does have a steady f*** buddy in married Tricia Walcott – sex with him which Bill believes is solely to fill her time – Bill doesn't date in having every expectation that Erica will return, he even setting a place for her at the Thanksgiving dinner table every year. Sam hasn't spoke to her mother in over a year in her hatred for her in blaming her for their parents' split. That split has resulted in Sam being a cynical young woman, who protects herself from being hurt by embarking on promiscuous sex with no strings. That cynicism is reflected in the novel she started writing after her parents' break-up, that novel which has just been published, her first published work. Louis, one of Sam's classmates who is unlike anyone she's ever slept with, tries to change Sam's perception of relationships between people as he pursues her romantically. Conversely, Bill doesn't feel that Rusty, who wants to be the next

Stephen King, has yet exposed himself enough to life to be a successful writer. As such, Rusty opens himself up in his pursuit of classmate Kate, part of the popular crowd and who has a boyfriend within that crowd, but she being a young woman with troubles of her own.

—Huggo

An accomplished author tries to hold on to his family of aspiring writers while dealing with his separation from his wife whom he still loves. Bill is a famous writer with a daughter, Sam, who is on the cusp of being published, and a son, Rusty, who is an aspiring suspense novelist. Bill is still reeling from the separation from his wife, Erica, who is now married to a younger guy. Sam and Rusty find his obsession of "reconciling" with his ex a delusion that is unhealthy for their dad's writing career. Bill is casually seeing a housewife on the side who advises him to get out there and start dating for real. Sam on the other hand, scarred by her mom's infidelity, remains hostile towards her mom, and acts out by being promiscuous and detached in her relationships. Rusty is in love with a troubled girl in school, who's in an abusive relationship and is an addict. When he rescues her from her boyfriend, he gets the girl of his dreams and starts writing successfully

Meanwhile, Sam meets an unassuming good boy Louis who wants a serious relationship. After hesitation, Louis makes Sam realize that love isn't so bad after all. Louis tries to reconcile Sam and Erica, to little success. As for Bill, when he starts to move on, Erica sees him in a better light and starts to love him again.

After a family crisis when Rusty's girlfriend is almost date-raped, Rusty retreats to being his aloof and guarded self and becomes depressed. He pulls through and starts to write again, gaining the attention of his favorite author, Stephen King. Louis' mom dies of cancer, which prompts Sam to re-evaluate her relationship with her mom. After turmoil, the family comes together and Bill and Erica reunite. The film ends with a thanksgiving dinner with the whole family in complete attendance.

Thanking You,

Sankalp Mirani

Contents

9 798887 494012

Printed by Libri Plureos GmbH in Hamburg,
Germany